How To Sell Any Home... Even the Hard To Sell

Alex Craig

Copyright © 2019 by Alex Craig All rights reserved. No part of this publication may be reproduced, distributed, or transmitted in any form or by any means, including photocopying, recording, or other electronic and mechanical methods, without prior written permission of the author, except in the case of brief quotations embodied in critical reviews and certain other noncommercial uses permitted by copyright law. For permission requests, write to the author, addressed "Attention: Permission Book", at the email address alexc@cb-hb.com.

All rights reserved.

ISBN: 9781799020127
ISBN-13: 9781799020127

DEDICATION

To my beautiful wife, Alexis, who has a gentle soul and is always supportive.

CONTENTS

	Introduction	1
1	Why Didn't My Home Sell?	17
2	The Formula for Selling Any Home… Even Yours	25
3	Crafting the Perfect Experience	39
4	M is for Marketing (Part 1): Building the Perfect Profile	55
5	M is for Marketing (Part 2): Promoting Your Home for Sale	78
6	Finding A Real Estate Agent	94
7	Building Your Pricing Strategy	103
8	A Special Invitation	111

INTRODUCTION

To sell your home, you need one thing to be present. Without it, selling your home is difficult, if not, near impossible. What is that one thing you need to be present? It's a motivated and qualified buyer. That's all it takes. Think about it for a second... it's a motivated and qualified buyer who buys a home. The motivated and qualified buyer has a strong desire to buy — often because of retirement, relocation, divorce, or some other life event that is forcing them to move — and the means to buy. Unmotivated buyers will look at homes all day long and never make an offer.

You might want to believe that it can't be that simple, but it is. All it takes is a motivated and qualified buyer. Everything you or your real estate agent does should generate and convert motivated and qualified home buyers. If your actions don't accomplish that task, then what you're doing is pointless. It's irrelevant and unnecessary to get your home sold.

If you can get a ton of qualified and motivated home buyers to tour your home, you can sell your home faster and for more money than similar homes in your neighborhood — even if your home isn't considered to be the most desirables because of its layout, location, or other factors. When you stop to think about it, the more eyeballs on your home, the higher our odds of getting an offer. Possibly multiple offers.

Motivated and qualified home buyers change the game of selling. You don't have to wonder why your home had few showings. No more rushing to clean your home after work before a 5:30pm showing and having to skip dinner for an unqualified home buyer that will never make an offer on your home. You can get rid of tire kickers so that when you leave your home for a showing, you're leaving with confidence. The confidence that your home will sell, and you will get an offer.

You might believe that it's the market that creates motivated and qualified home buyers. While it certainly influences the number of qualified home buyers, it's possible to find enough motivated and qualified home buyers in any market... even the worst real estate markets, like those in 2008 through 2012. I know this is true because homes sold that weren't foreclosures or short sales. Everyday-homeowners who had enough equity in their home wanted to sell and buy a new home on a discount. There were plenty of homes that needed to sell because of a divorce, and they sold to a motivated and qualified home buyer.

Homes that sell generate enough motivated and qualified home buyers, regardless of the market. They do this through a solid marketing plan built around the right pricing strategy. It's marketing that generates interest in your home and showings. It's pricing that converts the potential buyer into an actual buyer. You need to have both a solid marketing plan and the right pricing strategy. If you market, but have the wrong pricing strategy, you won't get offers. If you have the right pricing strategy and no marketing, you will struggle to get any showings.

In this book, we're going to layout our formula for generating tons of qualified and motivated home buyers who are kicking down your door practically begging to see it and make an offer. I'm going to show you how you can build a solid marketing plan built around the perfect strategy. Before I dive into all of that, I want to take a second to share with you why I wrote this book.

Why I Wrote This Book?

Sometimes things don't go right the first time, and that's okay. But, it's easy to give up on your dreams of selling. This book is likely in your hands because your home has "expired". It sat on the market for some time with a real estate and they were unable to get it sold. I know that when you list your home, you have ambitious dreams to get it sold in a couple of weeks for top dollar. On top of that, you hope you can keep the make the most amount of money and put it in your pocket.

Before you give up, I want you to read this book. I wrote this for the homeowner who has struggled to get their home sold but still as the deep desire and dream of selling their home. I wrote for the home seller who wants their home to sell but has been frustrated and disappointed with their real estate agent. I wanted to encourage you and any homeowner whose home did not sell the first time around. This book will be a source of confidence and encouragement for you if you decide to go out in try to get your home sold again.

You're likely going to hire a real estate agent again, and that's good. This book will give you the information you need to make a good hiring decision. It will also give you a scorecard to grade your real estate agent. I'm going to show you what makes a good marketing plan and how to develop your pricing strategy. If you see a real estate agent is meeting the requirements, I have laid out for a good marketing plan, then you know you need to change something if you want to get your home sold.

So, the first reason I wrote this book is to help every single homeowner, who wants to sell their home and failed the first time, get their home sold. I don't want you to give up on your dream so easily. If your dream is to move, I want to help you get there.

The second reason I wrote this book is because I wanted to live out my big hairy audacious goal (BAHG) of helping out every single homeowner in Michigan and the nation. Unfortunately, my resources, namely my time, is limited. Despite my best efforts, it's impossible for me to directly work with everyone. It's impossible for me to be able to be every homeowner's real estate agent. When I was young, my mother always told me that my ambition is always greater than my resources. At the time, I didn't really understand what she meant. Now that I'm older, trying to build my company and help as many people as I can, I get it. No matter how many resources I have, I will always lack resources for my dreams. As my resources expand, so do my dreams. Every time I achieve a dream I thought was beyond reality, I set my sights higher and believe more is possible. I've realized no matter how large or small my company is I will never have the resources need to help every homeowner directly.

Plus, I'm a licensed real estate agent in Michigan only. That means I can't directly help homeowners in New York, Texas or California. But I still have a deep to desire to. This book is a way of allowing me to do that. With the strategies I reveal in this book, I can help every homeowner who gets their hands on this book. It allows me to achieve my dream of helping every homeowner, without putting pressure on my time and resources.

The third reason I wrote this book is to create a guide for real estate agents. It's my hope that with this information real estate agents would be able to better serve their clients. I hope that many real estate agents will take this information and use it to help sell their clients home. This benefits the real estate because they can get more homes sold and increase their income. It benefits you because you get your home sold. You get a real estate agent who can get your home sold even if it didn't sell the first time.

You see, there are real estate agents out there that I call a "list and pray" agent. They put a sign in your yard, list your home on the multiple listing service, and then pray that someone else brings a home buyer. This isn't a good strategy. It takes a solid marketing plan built around a strong pricing to strategy to generate motivated and qualified home buyers to get your home sold. This book will give every agent tips and strategies for building a solid marketing plan and the right pricing strategy.

It's my hope that I can lead the industry like a Moses leading the Hebrews into the Promised Land. I want to metaphorically part the sea and reveal the dry land beneath so that every single real estate agent can cross the chasm that lies between listing a home and getting it sold. I want to lead both real estate agents and their clients to the Promised Land. This book acts as a guide to get there.

The reason I want to help real estate agents is because I have become increasingly concerned about the health of the real estate market. In a good real estate market, plenty of unqualified people are attracted to the real estate industry because of its perceived high-earning potential. A good real estate market can hide the quality and skill of a real estate agent. That's because homes will sell despite the lack of skill a real estate agent has.

It's only in a bad market that these people are flushed out and the quality of a real estate agent is revealed. As Warren Buffett famously said about investing, "Only when the tide goes out do you discover who has been swimming naked." When the market is good, a real estate agents' skills are hidden. The reality is the market will go down again and real estate agents who never learned to get a home sold won't be able to sell a home. If you're caught with one of these real estate agents when the market goes down, it's not going to be good for you.

That concerns me. I want this book to teach and give every real estate agent the skills they need to sell in a good market and a bad market. I don't want these real estate agents to be caught swimming naked because that means bad news for their clients.

What You Will Learn

This book is designed for the homeowner who wants to sell their home but couldn't the first time. It's written to take you from for sale to sold. Inside this book, I'm going to reveal all of the tips and tricks that you or your real estate agent needs to get your home sold — even if you think it's impossible, a bad real estate market, or you haven't had any luck.

First, we will walk through the reasons a home doesn't sell the first time around. You could probably come up with a ton of reasons, but you will learn that are really only two reasons your home doesn't sell. At the end of the day, everything is going to come down to pricing and marketing. Homes don't sell either because of a poor marketing plan or pricing strategy. I will share with you why this is and how to know if your home didn't sell because of marketing, pricing, or a combination of both. Why do you think your home didn't sell? Pricing or marketing?

For a majority of the book, I'm going to reveal my strategy for getting homes sold that other real estate agents couldn't. My strategy isn't some pie-in-the-sky theory but has been tested in the marketplace with dozens of home sellers. I have used this strategy over and over again to get homes sold that other real estate agents couldn't. I will dive deeper into how to craft the ultimate marketing plan that gets home buyers to stop dead in their tracks and grabs their attention by the throat long enough for them to look into your home and possibly tour it. You will also learn how to get in front of the most qualified and motivated buyers with one simple trick. Hint: it involves targeting the top real estate agents.

You learn how to create the perfect experience so that you can raise your home's market value, so you don't sell for less than it's worth. You're going to get your hands on some strategies you won't find anywhere else. That's because just like the founder of FedEx took the banking hub-and-spoke model and applied it to the logistics, I've taken strategies from the retail and hotel industry and have applied them to real estate. These strategies are unique to how we sell homes and you won't find them among other real estate agents — unless of course they have found their hands on my book.

Then, we will talk about how to hire the right real estate agent this time around. We will explore whether or not you should use the same real estate agent. I will share some things you should be on the lookout for when it comes to hiring a real estate agent. Lastly, we will end the book talking about pricing. Why would I wait until the end to share this information if the way to get a home sold is through a solid marketing plan built around the right pricing strategy? It's because homeowners get too focused on pricing. We believe pricing can be manipulated and fluctuate. The price you sell your home for will ultimately be affected by your marketing. The better your marketing, the higher you can sell it for. We will look at how to determine your home's value, and ultimately, how to set your pricing strategy.

One more thing, throughout this book, I will share stories of clients we have helped. Each story will be related to the chapter topic. I encourage you to read all of these to learn how we applied the exact strategies we're sharing to get a home sold. You might be able to imagine yourself in these situations. No doubt, some of these home sellers, will have stories similar to yours. These stories will show you how you can apply this information to get your home sold.

Why Should You Read This Book?

I know if I wasn't a real estate agent, reading a book about real estate agent wouldn't be on the top of my to-do list. It would be right up there next to reading a law book. One. Giant. Snooze fest. I suppose I might read a real estate book if I was having a hard time falling asleep. That's because most real estate books are filled with jargon that most people can't understand or they are just one giant self-promotional pitch.

For that reason, I have tried my very best to leave out all of the jargon and complicated talk that you often hear. You won't see any talk about FHA vs conventional. Whenever I'm forced to use jargon, I have tried to go out of my way to explain the word in simple terms that are easy to understand. I left out much of the "legal talk" because you can hire a real estate agent or attorney for help with the paperwork side of things. So, you really won't find a lot of that boring talk.

I have also tried to make sure this book contains value. There are a lot of real estate books on Amazon that are self-promotional pitches for that real estate agents service. These books don't contain any value or offer any real advice you can use to get your home sold. I understand that if you choose to read this book, there needs to be a fair exchange. If you are going to give me your time by reading this book, I want to make sure I am giving you something of equal value back. I want this to be worth your time. If I'm also going to kill a tree by printing this book, I want to make sure that it's creating value.

It's my sincere hope that I have lived up to this promise to provide value and make it simple. You be the judge and let me know. It's my serious intent to give you the exact tips and strategies you need to get your home sold without all of the fluff and bull-shit. That's why this book is short and condensed rather than 200+ pages.

Instead of focusing on the legal parts, this book is focused around marketing. That's because it's our fundamental belief that good marketing sells homes. It's good marketing that generates leads. It's also the skill set my company and I have developed over the last decade.

Lastly, this book wasn't written by a ghostwriter or somebody I hired off the internet, who has no real estate experience, to write this book. Everything you're going to read is written by me, Alex Craig, and has been tested in the marketplace. So, you know that these tips and tricks will work for you.

Why Should You Even Listen to Me?

Let me introduce myself. I'm Alex Craig, the founder of the Dolinski Group, a real estate agency team part of Coldwell Banker Hubbell-BriarWood in Lansing, Michigan (at the time of this writing). In 2016, I was a highly-paid marketing consultant in the telematics industry. I helped companies sell expensive technology solutions — often coming close to $50,000 — to Fortune 500 companies that needed help in the logistics and fleet management department.

HOW TO SELL ANY HOME... EVEN THE HARD TO SELL HOMES

But I decided to close my business down and transition into the real estate industry. I wanted to use my marketing skills and knowledge I had developed over the last decade to help homeowners, like yourself, get more exposure for their home, showings, more offers, and ultimately, get their home sold for more and faster than other real estate agents. When I looked into the real estate industry, I noticed it was filled with a lot of "list and pray" real estate agents who stick a sign in the yard, list the home on the multiple-listing service, and then pray that another real estate agent brings a qualified home buyer.

It seemed to me there were real estate agents who knew more about how to get home listed for sale than get a home sold through marketing. I got tired of seeing this, so I jumped into the real estate industry in an effort to bring a new standard when it came to marketing done for a client's home. I have used my skills to market clients' homes in every available marketing channel possible — from direct-mail, to Facebook Ads, to Google AdWords. All of this has allowed me to sell homes where other real estate agents have failed.

Selling a Home Other Agents Couldn't

"Alex is bright and personable. He has had tons of ideas to help us get

our home sold. *Very approachable and replies to questions quickly. We are very happy with Alex and will recommend him to everyone we know!"*

-Becky Turner; 10715 Bishop Hwy, Dimondale

SUCCESS STORY QUICK WINS

About Jim and Becky: After a series of health event, Jim and Becky decided it was time to sell their horse farm and move down to Florida — where they could relax and enjoy their retirement.

How We Helped Them Sell Their Home: When Jim and Becky decided to work with the Dolinski Group, their home had been listed on the market for five months with another real estate agent. To get is sold, we created a custom marketing plan — which included Facebook ads, Google AdWords, direct-mail, and more — that targeted as many horse owners as possible.

Results: It worked. In under three months we were able to get the property sold. Typical horse properties were taking five to six months to sell… even when properly marketed.

In the spring of 2017, Jim and Becky listed their home with a Lansing real estate agent who has traditionally been considered a "top real estate agent". Unfortunately, in five months, he wasn't able to sell the home. He had only 3 showings, and none of them were ever horse owners. Disappointed and frustrated by the results, or lack thereof, Jim and Becky decided to hire the Dolinski Group.

On A Time Crunch

It was the beginning of July when Jim and Becky contacted the Dolinski Group. When it came time to sit down with the couple to go over their objective, my team and I knew we were going to face a few massive hurdles. First, the couple wanted to sell their horse property before winter. If you know anything about the equestrian market, then you know that people stop buying horse properties by Thanksgiving. This meant we needed to sell the property before Thanksgiving.

The problem? The average horse property was taking six months to sell. It was already July. My team and I only had about four-and-a-half months to get it done. On top of that, how were we going to market a home that had been poorly listed by another real estate agent? We now had to explain and overcome the long days-on-market and price drops. But we were up for the challenge.

Our Custom Marketing Plan

First, we started by marketing the property on HorseProperties.net. Once on the site, my team and I ran a few experiments to get our listing to stand out in the search results. We found a few key elements that helped grabbed a buyer's attention and get people to click on our listing. First, we added a bright blue banner with some text. The bright blue was chosen so that it contrasted with the brown color palette of the website. It was guaranteed to stand out and capture a visitor's attention.

Second, our headline used special characters like asterisks. No other listings had these, so our listing was going to stand out. All of it worked. Our listing was one of the top performing listings on the website for a few weeks in a row. Meaning, we got some of the highest views and clicks.

Leveraging Social Media

To drive more traffic to our listing, my team and I decided to use Facebook because of its ability to target horse owners and a low cost. Of course, the analysis was a little bit more complex than that. When creating our Facebook ads, we targeted based on horse-related interests. Basically, anyone who liked topics like equestrian riding, horse riding, or horses was targeted. We wanted the right people to know about this home. For our ad, we decided to run a video ad. I took the aerial video my crew made.

Through Facebook ads, 3,348 people viewed the video for 10-seconds or more. The cost to me was $0.04 for every 10-second video view and a 16+% result rate to provide context, it's difficult to get any better than that. We were able to use Facebook to get really high results that most real estate agents would wish for and have no clue how to get. Imagine for $135, your home was guaranteed to be viewed by over 3,300 people. Who would you want listing your home?

Google AdWords Experiment

Honestly, when I set up the Google AdWords campaign, I wasn't expecting much. If any results. If you aren't familiar with Google AdWords, these are the ads that show up in Google when you search things. For example, when you search "Top Real Estate Agents", here are the ads that show up. Anywhere it says "ad", the company is using AdWords to advertise their website.

My team and I decided to take out and test a few ads for keywords like, "Horse Properties for Sale Michigan". I was shocked when the results came in. We had a 35+% click-through-rate. Meaning, for every 100 people that saw our ad,

> 35+% were clicking through to our website.
>
> To provide context, 3% is considered a good ad. We were getting 10x that. There were multiple reasons we got these results. We were able to leverage digital marketing platforms to show up in front of horse owners and get results for our client.
>
> **Our Marketing Was So Good That...**
>
> Our marketing was so good that it got the attention of a few real estate agents. One real estate agent in particular, who owned horses, reached out to me to let me know that our marketing was everywhere. She was being blasted and hit with our marketing. Everywhere she went, she saw our marketing for this property. Our results combined with this feedback from a real estate agent was validation that we nailed our marketing plan.
>
> And it all made a difference. In under three months, we were able to get an offer on the property. "If you want your house sold, then you really should hire Alex. He is a straight up guy, tells you like it is, and doesn't sugarcoat anything," said Jim. "I would hire Alex in a heartbeat."
>
> If you want to hear more about the story and you want to hear for your own words from Jim and Becky, you can watch our video at:
>
> **https://www.youtube.com/watch?v=CCFKp-yZHis**

If you're still looking for reasons why I'm qualified to be writing about selling a home, then do a simple Google search of me. You will find a ton of reviews and testimonials about the Dolinski Group's services. On top of that, I am one of the most reviewed real estate agents for Coldwell Banker in all of Michigan. That's not an easy accomplishment. You can also look throughout this book for all of our client stories to learn how we got their homes sold.

Key Messages of The Dolinski Group

You will find that the Dolinski Group takes a different approach to selling real estate than most agents. Our approach can almost be considered "radical". That's because my company is built on three foundational philosophies that you will find throughout this book.

Be Different, Almost Radical The way to win is to be different. There is this idea in sailing, it's called tick for tack. When you begin to head upwind with your boat and you're racing another boat. You have a decision to make; you can follow the lead boat's path and you will at least ensure that you remain the same distance behind them. Or you venture on your own path, where it is possible for you to take the lead. But you may risk losing. We believe that in this competitive landscape we have to be different. Many of the things we recommend are common sense, but very different than what you will see from other real estate agents. For example, marketing to other real estate agents is a common sense, but few real estate agents do it.

Transparency We believe an honest and trustworthy relationship can only happen when we are transparent. We have all been burned too many times. Communication is one of the things we prize because we want home sellers to know what is going on with their home. We don't want them to ever wonder what we're doing to get their home sold. I believe it's only through transparency that we can build lasting relationships. I have watched as some real estate agents withhold information, either to make a sale or so the seller needed the real estate agent. We believe that if information is the only value we can provide, then we have no point of being in business. Our value comes from applying the information we have.

Marketing first, everything else second. We believe marketing forms the foundation of getting a home sold. It's the most important thing. Without it, everything else is pretty much irrelevant. Your agent can be a skilled negotiator and even outfox a litigator, but all of it is irrelevant if a real estate agent can't generate qualified and motivated home buyers through marketing. We want to build our service and our business around a solid marketing plan that increases your chances of getting your home sold. Technology is changing the way we buy, so we invest a lot into digital marketing and marketing the home on the internet to get in front of my buyers.

While going through the book, you're likely to have questions. Be sure to write them on a separate sheet of paper or in the margins of this book. I'd love to help in any way that I can so when you have a question, be sure to reach out to me.

If you're in Lansing and looking to work with the Dolinski Group to get your home sold, you can get in touch with us by calling 734-752-2496 or sending an email to alexc@cb-hb.com. If you're outside of Lansing but still want your home sold, get in touch with me. You might qualify to work with a member of our extensive referral network. I can connect you with a real estate agent who shares these same principles and can help you get your home sold.

Alex Craig, founder of the Dolinski Group
www.dolinskigroup.com
alexc@cb-hb.com
734-752-2496

The Value of One Thing

One day I was listening to an audiobook called, 2-Second Lean. In the book, the author shared a strategy that he uses when he reads any book. Every time he is finished reading a book, he asks himself, "If I took one thing out of this book and seriously applied it to my life, what thing would have the biggest impact on my life and business?" And ever since, I have tried to do the same thing.

There are hundreds of things that you can do to get your home sold. I'm going to reveal a ton of tips and tricks. The list of things "to do" to get your home sold, can quickly become overwhelming. The long list can seem like a barrier, which prevents you from doing anything. For that reason, at the end of every chapter, I want to give one thing, that if seriously applied, would make a huge difference in getting your home sold. These will be a summary of the main point that I want you to take away from this book. And when applied, will help you get your home sold.

ONE THING

Homes that generate qualified and motivated home buyers, and ultimately sell, are built around a solid marketing plan with the right pricing strategy. How does your marketing and pricing strategy stack up?

---

1 Why Didn't My Home Sell?

You can probably come up with a long list of reasons your home didn't sell. Shoot, I'm sure you've already generated this list in your head while you were up late at night, unable to fall asleep because your home hasn't sold. Despite the length of your list, there are really only two reasons a home doesn't sell. Not one-thousand. Not one-hundred. Not even ten. Just two.

The two reasons a home doesn't sell are because of pricing and marketing. Every reason you come up with can fit into those two categories. Not enough showings? A result of your marketing. No offers? Likely a result of your pricing or a combination of both. Think it's because your home is unique? Likely an issue with your marketing. Every single reason is likely the result of a poor marketing plan, the wrong pricing strategy, or a combination of both.

But What About the Real Estate Market?

Whenever I share the idea that there are only two reasons a home doesn't sell, I get a little bit of resistance. Part of it's because homeowners can't believe it's that simple. The other part is because they want to believe external circumstances, like the real estate market, can be blamed for why a house doesn't sell. For example, it's easy to blame the real estate market in a buyer's market. When this happens, you abdicate responsibility and control when it comes to selling your home. Instead, you believe it's up to the market, and that's just not true.

It doesn't matter how the market is performing — whether it's the worst recession you have seen, or the market is at an all-time high. Your home won't sell because of marketing or pricing. There is always a solid marketing plan that you can build around the right pricing strategy that will get your home sold in any market. I know this to be true because plenty of homes sold through 2008 and 2012 that weren't foreclosures or short sales. It was everyday home owners who wanted to get out of their homes and move into something different.

The problem people have is that the pricing might not be what people are willing to accept. In a buyer's market, I often see the wrong pricing strategies and homes that are overpriced. The average homeowner has very little equity in a home, so when the market goes down, it's common for homeowners to need more for their home than it can sell for. So, in a bad market, it's often a pricing issue if your home doesn't sell.

It doesn't matter how the economy is doing or any external circumstances that arise. It doesn't matter if the Federal Reserve is raising interest rates and driving out all of the home buyers in the market. It doesn't matter what Trump is doing as President. It doesn't matter if the economy is going and unemployment is on the rise. The only issue with these circumstances is if they create unfavorable conditions for you to sell at. I can assure you that there is a marketing plan and pricing strategy that will get any home sold in any market.

Is It Pricing or Marketing?

Hopefully by now I've convinced you that there are really only two reasons a home doesn't sell. It really is only because of marketing and pricing. So, at this point, you might be wondering what's the reason MY home isn't selling? If you can figure out why your home isn't selling, then you can set about creating a strategy for getting your home sold. For example, if you know a home has the wrong pricing strategy, you can lower the price. If it's the marketing, then you can create a new marketing plan or find a new real estate agent to create a better marketing plan than the one you previously had.

The answer to the question is pretty simple and it lies in your data. You need to know how long your house was listed, how many showings you had during that time frame, and if you had any offers. We look at the number of showings within our given time frame and then compare that to what we're seeing in the industry. If our showings are below average, we have a marketing issue. This makes sense because we are attracting less home buyers than other homes on the market. It means the home isn't getting in front of home buyers and is drowning in the sea of listings on Zillow.

To find a pricing issue, we will take our number of offers given our number of showings and compare it to market average. In any given market, we expect a certain number of offers given our showings. For example, in a balanced market, we often expect one offer for every eight showings. In a seller's market, this number is often much lower. In a bad buyer's market, like 2008 through 2012, this number creeped up closer to one offer for every 20 showings. So, if you had showings and no offers, then you have a pricing issue. That's because people don't like the terms of our home. We got people to tour, but nobody wanted to buy it given our current terms.

It's important to understand that these metrics we expect to see can be market specific, and not just the economy. They are also geographically specific. They are price specific. For example, just because of the nature of the luxury market, we often expect very few showings over a long period of time. The luxury market isn't that large. Not many people can afford a home that is in the top ten percent of values in their area. They are also specific to the home. For example, when we listed a horse property, the average home was getting an offer every six showings. But because our market was a bit more niche and horse owners look for properties that fit their exact needs, we knew we would get an offer after around 15 showings.

When you're looking for these numbers, the only way to really find them is through a real estate agent. They should be able to give you an idea of these metrics based on your home's value, the area, and the market. These metrics should be the benchmark you use to evaluate your real estate agent, even after they are hired. If the market is seeing eight showings in two months, and your home has been on the market for three months with two showings, then you can realize early on that you have a marketing issue. You can take corrective action before your home doesn't sell.

Often times, bad marketing is easy to identify. It's intuitive. I think every single homeowner knows bad marketing from good marketing. You can look at your photos and know how they compare to other listings. You can see if they are better or worse than market average. Really, you hardly need to look at your numbers. Pricing, on the other hand, requires metrics. As a result, I often find homeowners have questions around pricing. They try to find out if they have a pricing issue through other methods. One common method is looking at your neighbor's home to see if you have a pricing issue or not.

Yeah, But My Neighbor's Home...

Ahhh, the good ol' neighbor. The bane of my existence as a real estate agent. We all want to compare our home to our neighbor's home. When we're wondering about our pricing, we look around at our neighbor's home. We see their home sold for the price we're asking or maybe even higher. So, there is good reason to believe ours should sell for our neighbor's price. I mean, our home is better after all, right?

Sometimes, you might be right. There could be a good chance that your neighbor's home is a perfect comparable to yours. If that's the case, and your home is underpriced and still not selling, then you have an issue with your appraised value and market value. We will address that issue in the next section of this chapter. For a majority of homeowners though, your neighbor's home is usually a bad comparable.

Comparing your home to other similar homes is the only way to truly determine your home's right price. There is a good chance your home isn't exactly like every other on the block. You want to look for homes that are most similar to yours and then you will need to make pricing adjustments for any differences. For example, if your neighbor's home sold for more, it could be because it has more square footage or an extra garage.

As real estate agents, we might call this a comparable market analysis. It's where we look at what comparable homes have sold for over the last six months and come up with a price. Most homeowners have no issues finding comparable homes, but adjustments are important. Adjustments reveal a home's true price. That's why it's not enough to just look at what your neighbor's home sold for.

Let's say that you or a real estate agent did a comparable market analysis. You looked at your neighbor's home and made adjustments. You found out that your home is worth more than the price you had it listed at and it still didn't sell. That's where we have a difference between our appraised value and our market value. Let's address this issue.

My Home Is Underpriced and It Still Didn't Sell

Every so often I have a dialogue with a homeowner that goes like this. "Listen, Alex, my home is underpriced compared to what every real estate agent is telling me and what I have seen on Zillow, but my home still hasn't sold. What gives?" And that's a great question. It gives me a chance to talk about psychology and human behavior.

If your home is underpriced when compared to its appraised value, there is an issue between your market value and appraised value. Let me define these terms quickly. You may hear the term market value and appraised value thrown around interchangeably. But they are something different. In an ideal world, market value and appraised value are the same. You may also hear people define the market value as the price the home sells for. But this definition excludes homes that don't sell. Instead, we define the market value as what a buyer is willing to pay. The appraised value is what the bank, an appraiser, or real estate agent says it's worth from doing a comparable market analysis.

When your home is listed under its appraised value and still not selling, then you have an issue with your market value. The market value of your home is lower than the appraised value. In other words, buyers are not willing to pay what you're asking. There could be several reasons for this, but common reasons include, too many days on the market, a bad showing experience, or poor marketing.

Here's how this plays out in the real world. Let's say your home is worth $200,000 according to an appraiser. Your home was listed on the market for the last six months at $190,000 and it still didn't sell. The market is telling you that they aren't willing to pay even $190,000 for your home. To get your home sold at this point, you have two options. First, you can drop the home's price to match what the market is willing to pay, or you can try to increase your home's market value. In the chapter about experience and marketing, we look at several ways you can increase a home's market value. We will even show you how to push your home's market value beyond your home's appraised value — allowing you to get more for you home than it's worth.

So, whenever you have a pricing issue, it means your pricing is higher than what the market is willing to pay. It's important to understand that what the market is willing to pay is in constant fluctuation and influenced by many factors, like days on market, the marketing, and the experience. Your home's market value is all about perception. The appraised value is about reality. The perception of value is just as important, if not more important, than the real value. Your home is worth it's appraised value, but if the market doesn't believe it's worth the appraised value, it's going to sell for less. And that's an important key learning experience.

Do I Need More Time?

Before I end this chapter, I want to address one more common question. It's possible for your home to become an expired listing even if you have a strong marketing plan built around a solid pricing strategy. To understand this, it helps by defining what an expired listing is. An expired listing happens when your home doesn't sell within the date that was put in your original list agreement with your real estate agent. For example, let's say you list your home on January 25th. The listing agreement is for six months. So, you have until July 25th to get your home sold. If the date passes, your listing agreement becomes null and void and your home is considered an expired listing.

Just because you're an expired listing, it doesn't mean you have a pricing or marketing issues. Remember, to find out if we have a marketing or pricing issue, we need to look at the number of tours we had and if we had any offers during our listing period. Then, we need to compare that to the market average.

So, it begs the question, "how do you know if you just need to give your home more time to sell?" For that, we need to look at what we call average days on market, or DOM. If the average DOM for homes like yours is eight months and you sign a six-month agreement with your real estate agent, then there is a good chance your home will expire before it sells. If you're getting the average number of showings the rest of the market is experiencing, then you don't have any marketing issue. You just need to give your home more time to sell.

To find the average days on market, take a look at comparable homes. How long did they take to sell? This will give you a starting benchmark for deciding if you need to give your home more time to sell or if you really do have a marketing and pricing issue. Your DOM is going to be specific to the conditions of the real estate market, your geography, and your price point. For example, it's common for luxury homes to take anywhere from two to three times longer to sell than a home priced at the median value.

Just because your home expires does not mean that there is anything wrong with it. However, if you aren't hitting the market's showing benchmark or offer-to-showing ratio, then you likely have a pricing and marketing issues. If you're hitting these metrics and your home has been listed less than the average DOM, then you just need to give it more time.

ONE THING

Your home's market value is all about perception. The appraised value is about reality. The perception of value is just as important, if not more important, than the real value. Your home is worth it's appraised value, but if the market doesn't believe it's worth the appraised, then it's going to sell for less.

2 THE FORMULA FOR SELLING ANY HOME… EVEN YOURS

How do you sell a home that has been sitting on the market for the last six months, without dropping its price? That's the question I asked myself over and over again. It's common to relist a home and just drop the price. Remember, to get a home sold, our asking price needs to align with the market value, or what the market is willing to pay. We could do that by dropping the price or increasing what the market is willing to pay. It's much easier to drop the price, but this less money to a home seller. Plus, I find that a certain percentage of the homes are already below its appraised value. But how can you get a home sold that's been on the market for some time without dropping its price?

In this chapter, I'm going to reveal my formula for getting any home sold. This formula answers the questions and presents strategies for getting your home sold without having to sacrifice our price position. Of course, if we're higher than the appraised value, then we will need to lower the price. The formula can't guarantee the sale of your home, but it can increase your odds. It gives you the best chance of selling your home. The strategies I am going to share with you aren't theory or written because they sounded good in a book. All of these strategies are tested and what we use every day to get homes sold that other real estate agents couldn't. With that said, let me introduce you to our TEAM formula.

What Is Your TEAM Formula?

Our TEAM formula is what we use every day to sell homes — regardless of how long they have been on the market, whether they're a brand-new listing, or have been on the market for months. The TEAM formula is a handy acronym that stands for terms, experience, abode, and marketing. We use these four elements to look at a property holistically and to develop the best strategy for getting a home sold. Each element is important and needs to be considered in order to get a home sold. The exclusion of just one of these elements could prevent a home from selling.

Real briefly, I'm going to define each element and then in the subsequent chapters, we will dive deeper into the specific strategies and tactics within each element so that you can get your home sold. For now, let's take a look at our TEAM formula from a high-level.

The first element, T, stands for terms. This includes everything we are asking for in order to sell our home. The most common component is our asking price, or how much we want to sell our home for. It also includes any other terms we need to make the deal. For example, we may need a buyer with specific loan terms such as cash or conventional. We may need 15 to 30 days occupancy of the home after close so that you have time to move. By far, the most important term is pricing. We talked a lot about pricing in Chapter 1, and we have also devoted a chapter near the end to explore pricing further.

The E is for experience. This is defined as what the process of dealing with your home is like — for both the real estate agent and the home buyer. For example, what is it like to tour your home? Was it easy and convenient to set up a showing or did it take a lot of effort? What does your home look like when a buyer is taking a tour? Is cluttered and a mess or is it clean and simple?

The experience you create will influence your home's market value. A good experience will lead to a higher market value, and buyers who are willing to pay more. A bad experience will hurt your chances of selling and lower the amount buyers are willing to pay for your home. We will go into several tactics and strategies for improving your experience, but for now, I want you to think about what it's like as a home buyer to tour your home? It's not enough for your experience to be mediocre or even average. It needs to be exceptional. It needs to be among the best on the market.

The third element, A, stands for abode. It's your home. It's the thing you're trying to sell. It's a 3-bedroom home with two bathrooms. It's the style of your home — ranch, bi-level, or two-story. There really isn't much we can change about your home, aside from things like painting, which falls under your experience. We include this element in our formula because we have to look at the home you're trying to sell. It will influence our pricing as well as our marketing. For example, if you have a horse property, then that influences our ideal target market. The home you have will always affect the market that we target.

Quick Note on Fair Housing Laws

As a marketer, targeting groups of people who are likely to buy your home is one of the best ways to get your home sold. But we have to be very careful. Did you know marketing only to specific groups — Millennials, Latinos, and Baby Boomers — and not marketing to others, may be a violation of Fair Housing Laws? Whenever there is a disproportional ad spend targeting a specific market, it's possible we can be in violation of Fair Housing Laws. For example, if we create a large marketing budget targeting Millennials and reserve limited funds for other age groups.

> When we are looking to target a specific market, we have to make sure that it's not based on characteristics that the Fair Housing Laws are set up to protect. For example, we can't target a market based on race, color, religion, sex, national origin, familial status, disability, age, or marital status. Whenever we are targeting our marketing, we look instead for interests. For example, when we had a horse property for sale, we targeted horse owners and anyone with interest in horses. When we had an investment property, we targeted the general market and set up a campaign to target people who had an interest in real estate investing through their actions on Facebook.

M is for Marketing. The marketing element is broken down into two categories — our listing profile and the promotion of the home. In other words, how does your home look on sites like Zillow, the Multiple-Listing Service, and Realtor.com? Then, how are we getting home buyers to view your profile? The goal of your listing profile is to generate interest and ideally a conversion (defined as a lead captured or a home buyer taking a tour of your home). The goal of promotion is to let every single homeowner know that your home is for sale. We can often measure it by the total views or traffic to your listing profile or the number of people saving your home in their search results.

Both the profile and promotion are important. It's not enough to just build a solid listing profile. Build a good profile without promoting the home is like the old question, "if a tree falls down and nobody is around to hear it, does it make a noise?" Without a promotional plan, you're hoping that Zillow ranks your profile or that it stands out in the sea of thousands of listings. There needs to be an active approach in your marketing plan to make sure that real estate agents and home buyers know that your property is for sale. We will explore several strategies for building a strong listing profile and creating a promotional plan in a later chapter.

Selling and Buying A Home At The Same Time

"To find a realtor who does not pressure their clients into a sale to make a quick dollar is hard to come by. You will not be pressured by Alex. He will assist you with the decision making, but ultimately leaves the decisions to you. I highly recommend Alex, not just for his trustworthiness as a professional, but to also have a good friendly relationship with his clients. He is prompt with following back with his clients as well. He listened to our needs and was able to show us homes within our budget. Our overall experience with Alex has been fantastic, and I feel comfortable giving him 5 stars knowing he will be able to assist you as well."

-Holly F.; Holt, MI

SUCCESS STORY QUICK WINS

About Matthew and Holly: They decided it was time to move out into the country, but they needed to be able to sell their house first before they could buy. This is tough to do in a seller's market.

How We Helped Sell Their Home: We did everything to create the best listing profile, and that meant professional photos and aerial photos. On sites like Zillow, our listing performed far better than the average home.

Results: In under 30 days, we received a ton of showings and 3 offers. We accepted a full-price offer.

Having lived in a subdivision for years, and giving it a lot of thought, Matthew and Holly decided it was time to pack up and move out to the country. They wanted more space and they knew it would be good for their son, who has autism.

When I first met Matthew and Holly at an open house, they were just starting their journey. It had been awhile since they purchased a home, so they weren't certain how long it would take a home like theirs to sell, how much their home might be worth, and how tough the market is for buyers. I took the time to listen to what they were trying to accomplish and created a custom solution. "He listened to our needs and was able to show us homes within our budget," said Holly

Holly and Matthew would need to be able to sell their home first, then use the equity in their home to purchase a new one. One problem… this is difficult to do in a seller's market. First, many home sellers will reject or counter an offer that is dependent on a buyer being able to sell their home. There is too much perceived risk on the seller's part.

Second, once my clients sold their home, they had a short time to buy a home. Or they would find themselves needing to find a short-term living situation, which would have been bad with their son. To make a difficult task more difficult, they needed the timing to be perfect. They needed to close around the end of May or beginning of June so they didn't have a long time they would have to drive their kids to school. I was up for the challenge and worked hard to get it done perfectly.

Getting Our Offers Rejected

Getting an offer accepted that is dependent on selling a buyer's home is difficult when most homes are getting multiple offers over asking price. It can be done, but home sellers usually prefer a buyer's home to have an accepted offer on it.

That didn't deter us. We wrote a few offers. I was hopeful that, by chance, we would get one of our offers accepted by improving other terms of a purchase agreement. For example, we increased the offer price and the earnest money deposit, so sellers took us serious. It would have been ideal for my clients to get an offer accepted before they sold their home. But we had no luck.

The market and price point where my clients wanted to buy was too competitive. We were going to need to change gears and get their home sold. It was disappointing to lose out on some of the homes, but we wanted to avoid the stress that comes from selling your home first. Once you sell your home, you have limited time to find a new home. And this can be challenging when there are a small number of homes listed on the market.

"To find a realtor who does not pressure their clients into a sale to make a quick dollar is hard to come by. You will not be pressured by Alex. He will assist you with the decision making, but ultimately leaves the decisions to you," said Holly

Shifting Gears: Getting the Home Sold

Selling any home starts with a great listing profile. And that's what we created. Homes with aerial photos sell more than 60 percent faster than homes without aerial photos. So, we had a professional photographer, like we do on most listings, take photos and include some aerial shots. We had over 30 photos that we posted to our listing profile. This is important because, from internal data, listings with over 30 photos perform better — in terms of views and saves — than similar listings.

As a result, we were able to get our listing profile to outperform many similar listings on Zillow. In fact, we were getting nearly double the results. In under 30 days, we were able to schedule over 20 showings and get 3 offers. Holly and Matthew accepted a full-price offer.

The Clock Was Ticking

Once we had an accepted offer on their home, the clock began ticking. We needed to find them a home or risk leaving them in limbo. If they got caught in limbo, they would need to find a temporary living arrangement, which would have caused a lot of disruption and stress on their son. "Alex made the buying and selling process easy by making sure we sold our house, bought a new house, and the new people could move into the house they just bought all almost at the same time," said Matthew.

Within a week, we found their dream home. But it was going to be a multiple offer situation. How could we write the best offer, even though the offer needed to be dependent on my clients' ability to close on their home? We did the usual; asked at asking price, submitted a large earnest money deposit, and more. But it was one simple tactic I recommend to buyers that allowed us to win. My clients wrote a letter to the sellers. It's easy to dismiss this strategy and think it doesn't matter. But when done right, it can make a huge difference. The key is to bring emotions and an element of humanity to your offer. This way, home sellers are no longer just looking at the numbers.

Can We Time It Right?
We managed to get an offer on their home and find a new home, where the closing would be June 1st. Perfect since school would be finishing up near that time. Now it was about managing all of the paperwork to make sure we closed on time. About three weeks before closing, the seller of the home Holly and Matthew wanted to buy wanted to push closing to a week later.

That wasn't going to be possible. We needed to close on the 1st or my clients wouldn't have anywhere to live. We stuck to the closing dates. Tension rose as we moved closer to the expected closing date. That's because about a week before closing we had received the clear to close on the sale of Matthew and Holly's house, but we were waiting on the home they wanted to buy. I began following up with everyone and getting everyone to push this faster so that we closed on time.

In the end, we were able to close on the same day. And we were able to do it with minimal problems, aside from the little uncertainty of whether we would be able to get the clear to close. It could have been much worse.

Yes, it was a stressful process for Holly and Matthew, but in the end, it was all worth it. "I highly recommend Alex, not just for his trustworthiness as a professional, but to also have a good friendly relationship with his clients. He is

> prompt with following back with his clients as well," said Holly. "Our overall experience with Alex has been fantastic, and I feel comfortable giving him 5 stars knowing he will be able to assist you as well."

The Challenges of An "Expired" Home

There are some unique challenges in selling a home that has been on the market for a while. Before you can understand what makes our formula a perfect solution for getting your home sold, you have to understand these challenges. There are three of them.

Market History. This is probably the biggest challenge. Your home has a market history. Home buyers can see that your home has been on the market for six months, three months, or a year. You might think the solution is to delist it, and then list it a few months from now. It will still have a market history that buyers can see. From talking to home buyers, I can guarantee you every single buyer is looking at your home's market history. If you had issues trying to sell it in the past, what you bought it for, and the last time it was sold. This market history is something we often have to overcome because a poor market history will decrease the buyer's perception, lowering what they are willing to pay. Crafting the perfect experience allows us to increase the market value and a buyer's perception. It allows us to overcome the market's negative perception of the home.

Pricing Issues. The agent that originally listed the horse property — Jim and Becky's — started the asking price at $374,000. Five months later, when I took the listing, he had lowered the price to $297,000. From doing a market analysis, I determined the home was worth around $325,000. This home had a major pricing issue and was a perfect example of a home not selling even though it's far below its appraised value. I had to have a hard discussion with the home sellers. Do we raise the price back to its appraised value and then overcome the market's objections and concerns over the price increase? Or do we keep it where it is and end up selling the home for less than appraised value but at least it's better perceived by the market? Expired homes often have pricing issues, and this will affect the market's perception. Our pricing strategy, under the TEAM formula, allows us to address any pricing issues that a home may have.

Lack of Home Buyers. When you list your home for the first time, you have the ability to get the interest of every single home buyer. As your home sits on the market, your chance of getting the attention of a home buyer decreases. Most of the traffic that visits your listing profile or tours your home will be new home buyers entering the market. That's why we see most of the traffic for a home in the first 30 days and then it slowly tapers off. A majority of the home buyer market will have already seen your home and written it off. Our marketing plan will combat this by getting your home in front of new home buyers, real estate agents, and the existing home buyer market. By showing up frequently, we can get home buyers to reconsider our home.

Our TEAM formula is perfect for overcoming every challenge that faces and expired listing. It's a perfect formula for getting any home sold. Before I dive into our formula any further, I want to talk about how it was developed, why I know it works, and how these elements interact.

How Do You Know It Works?

When I was looking for the perfect formula or a framework to use to get homes sold, I did a ton of research. Part of that research involved studying companies like Apple and Nike, who sold billions of dollars worth in products. If there was a company that could teach me about selling, it had to be these companies. Now, I know they have little to do with real estate. I mean, one sells shoes and another technology solution. How could they possibly relate enough to teach me?

What I discovered was a framework that these companies use to sell products. It's called the 4P's of Marketing. It stands for

Product, Price, Promotion, and Placement. Product, the first of the 4P's, is the good or intangible service you're selling. Once you have an understanding of your product, you can start making pricing decisions. With a product and price, you can begin looking at ways to market the product. The last element, placement, is about where people can purchase your product. It was after learning these four elements that I realized I could apply much of this to real estate. If Apple and Nike could use it to sell billions of dollars worth of products, certainly I could adapt and modify it to sell millions of dollars worth of real estate. And that's exactly what I did.

When you look at the 4P's of Marketing, you can see how much of our TEAM formula ties into it. For example, the first P, or product, is aligned with the Abode. It's the thing that we are selling. Your home is our product. Of course, pricing and pricing are directly aligned under our term's element. Then, promotion is marketing. The M in our TEAM formula. The only one that didn't align was placement. We can't change the location of a home. It's fixed. So, we substituted placement for experience. The placement didn't apply to real estate and we felt like the experience was the next most important element to getting a home sold.

Next, we needed to apply this formula. I didn't want it to only work in theory. From the day I started as a real estate agent, I applied the formula. I have used it to sell over a million dollars worth in real estate. It turned out this formula was perfect for getting a home sold. To this day, we are constantly refined the strategies within our formula, but the formula seems to be standing the test of time. We will continue to test and optimize our formula to make it the best it can be. As the market shifts, so do our strategies within our formula.

How the Elements of TEAM Interact?

When it comes to the TEAM formula, these elements interact to balance each other. But, it's not perfectly distributed. Instead, on one side, you have the terms you're asking for, most notably your price. On the other side, you have the experience you craft, your marketing, and your home. These elements interact like a seesaw. To get your home sold, you want them to be perfectly balanced. When they are perfectly balanced, your home sells for the best price possible — netting you the most money in your pocket. It helps to understand what happens when the seesaw is unbalanced to understand why a balanced seesaw is import and the optimal outcome.

There are two situations where a seesaw is unbalanced. Either, the terms outweigh the experience you're crafting, the marketing, and your home. Or, your experience, marketing and home outweigh your terms. When your terms outweigh your experience, marketing, and home, your home is overpriced, and it won't sell. Your experience, marketing, and home all work to increase the market's perceived value. When your terms are too heavy, your marketing, experience and home aren't doing enough to raise its perceived value. To get it back to balance, and get your home sold, you either need to lower your price or improve your marketing, experience, and home.

Let's look at the opposite situation. If your experience, marketing and abode outweigh your terms, then you're going to sell your home for less than you could have. You're going to leave money on the table. When your marketing, experience and abode weigh more than your terms, you're selling your home for less than what the market was willing to pay. Your solution is to increase pricing. By increasing pricing, you're ensuring you're getting the most for your home.

So, it's balanced seesaw, or a balance between your terms, marketing, experience, and abode that will allow you to get your home sold and net the most amount of money in your pocket. The higher your terms, the more you need to focus on your marketing, experience, and abode. Whatever price you decide for your home, you need to make sure your marketing, experience and abode match. Otherwise, you risk leaving money on the table or risk having your home sit on the market.

ONE THING

Through marketing and experience, focus on increasing your home's market value and the perception that home buyers have. Make sure your asking price is balanced with your experience, marketing, and abode.

3 CRAFTING THE PERFECT EXPERIENCE

In this chapter, we're going to talk about how to craft the perfect experience. The experience you create will have the biggest influence on what the market is willing to pay for your home. Through your experience, you will also increase the chances that your home sells. Before we dive into some strategies for crafting the perfect experience, I want to define it. The experience is how you affect a home buyers' perception of your home's value through seeing, doing, and feeling. But it runs deeper than the home buyer. It's also the experience of the real estate agent. It's not about affecting its home's value but if the transaction will be worth it.

So, when we're talking about the experience, we are talking about any moment a home buyer interacts with your home — from its listing profile, to the photos, to the moment they tour the home. The experience really involves any interaction that somebody has, regardless of the medium, with your home.

Why Build An Experience For The Home Buyer And The Agent?

For home buyers, it makes sense to build an experience. Throughout this book, I've already highlighted many of the benefits to creating for a home buyer — increased perceived value so you can sell your home for more and faster. What's not so obvious is why you should create the perfect experience for a real estate agent, too. In fact, most homeowners and real estate agents don't even think about how to build an experience for a buyer's real estate agent. I think it's because we often think they're not the one buying the home. This is true, but we still need to be able to sell them on the transaction. We want the real estate agent to believe that this transaction will be smooth and will go well.

Creating an experience that communicates the message to the real estate agent that this will be a great transaction is important and that this home is worth it. First, a real estate agent that believes the home's asking price is aligned with its market value, will advocate on your behalf. In other words, you will have another real estate agent who is working just as hard to sell your home. They will work hard to overcome objections a buyer may have and to get the home buyer to write an offer. If for some reason, this buyer isn't a good fit, there is a chance that the real estate agent may promote the home to their other buyers. By building an experience that increases the perceived value of your home will go a long way in getting other real estate agents to sell your home. They will see it as a deal and will want to get their buyers into the home. It benefits these real estate agents to show them homes where the perceived value is high. Everyone wins.

You also want to communicate that the transaction will be smooth. This will be dependent on your real estate agent. It's important to understand this when you hire your real estate agent. I know it's not really considered, but your real estate agent will affect whether people write offers or not. If a buyer's agent thinks doing a transaction with the selling agent or homeowner will be difficult, they will look elsewhere or offer a lower price and call it a "hassle discount". Dealing with you is going to be difficult so we're going to offer a lower home price. If you want a buyer's real estate agent to believe the transaction will be smooth, then they need to have a smooth experience. Scheduling a home showing must be easy. It must be easy for the buyer's agent to get ahold of the real estate agent that has your home listed. I know this is true because I have been that home buyer. I have advised my clients about the difficult of the deal and many times they just don't want to bother.

So, what does the experience for a real estate agent look like? From the moment a buyer's agent see your home, to the moment they schedule a showing, to the moment they are touring a home, all of it needs to be easy and convenient. The moment anything is made more difficult than it needs to be, or obstacles are put in place, is the moment you create a bad experience for the real estate agent.

Let's look at a few ways real estate agents and homeowners create bad experiences without realizing it. One that commonly arises happens because of safety concerns. That's the location of the lockbox, where the keys are held. I have had real estate agents hide the lockbox, so when I get to the property, I have to go hunt for the box.

I will never forget one property, in particular, that I toured. The lockbox was located in the backyard. So, when we arrived we had to walk from the front of the house through to the backyard. No big deal, right? It wasn't. But the lockbox was hidden. I was told it's on a chair near the door. I was touring the home at 6pm in the middle of winter so it's dark out, the chair the box hung on was black, and the box was black. Talk about a tough find.

When I finally found the box, I grabbed the keys. It happened to be a warmer night when I was touring the home, so much of the snow and ice from the previous week was melting. There were icicles right above the door that were melting. In order for me to open the door, the water had to drip on me. In order for my clients to get through the door, they would need to walk through the water.

Before I or my buyer stepped in the home, we already had a bad experience and that shaped how we toured the home. These things are subtle, and something most people don't think about. Sure, the seller couldn't control the weather, but they could have solved the issue by putting the lockbox on the front door. You have to weigh what's more important, the experience you create or addressing safety concerns.

Another differentiator between a good experience and a bad experience can be technology, or the lack of use. When it comes to scheduling a showing for a home, it should be easy. It's best to do all of this online through automated scheduling software. This way, all a real estate agent has to do is click a few buttons and wait for confirmation to tour the home. If we make a real estate agent call and jump over hoops to schedule a showing, they will perceive the transaction will be the same. It will be difficult and hard to complete.

Okay, hopefully you see the importance of creating an experience for the buyer's agent. With all of that said, let's shift our focus to how you can create the perfect experience for the home buyer. Our experience needs to sell the dream. We need to sell the dream of living there in the lifestyle of that. What follows in the rest of this chapter is strategies for doing just that.

The Luxury Home Selling Strategy to Net 15% More

Maybe you don't own a home that would conventionally be considered expensive, but I want you to imagine for a second that you are the proud owner of a three-million-dollar home, and you're trying to sell it. Whether you're using a real estate agent or not is irrelevant. You have this three-million-dollar home and you need to sell it so you can move on with your life.

Running a few simple calculations, I want you to see how small changes can result in big outcomes. If you could sell your three-million-dollar home for just one percent more, how much more money would you net? On a three-million-dollar sale, an extra one percent, just one percent, translates into $30,000.

It's reasonably safe to assume that if you knew there was a strategy for increasing the sale of your home by one percent, you would do it, right? The market that is traditionally considered to be affluent or part of the luxury market has figured out how to do exactly that. They have figured out a strategy for increasing their home's value by one, two, five, and even 10 percent more — allowing them to net tens to hundreds of thousands of dollars.

So, what's this one strategy that the luxury market is using to net at least 15 percent more in their pocket? It's the art of home staging. That's it. Before I make the case and show you the data that supports my claim that staging can make you more money, I need to define it. It's not just staging that works. It's the right kind of staging.

When I say staging, a lot of people just think it's about putting furniture and decor in the home. Let me be clear what staging really is and what it is not. While furniture and decor are part of it, that's not the whole story. Staging a home is about creating an environment that encourages buyers to come see it and gets them to make an offer. It's about telling a story and creating a dream for the buyer — one where they can imagine living in your home. The story you're telling has to align with the aspirations of a specific buyer.

For example, if you're selling a condo that would be well-suited for a single male, staging the home with a kid's room and family-oriented decor would be inappropriate. It would tell the wrong story. But if you're selling a home that would be perfect for the growing family, then it makes sense to stage the home with a kid's playroom. If you have a starter home, think about a nursery. Telling the right story is important and it can help you get your home sold faster and for more money.

To get the most out of staging, it starts with understanding who your market is. What kind of market is most likely to buy your home? Second, you need to know what kind of lifestyle that person wants to live. Then, you have to set about creating that environment in your home. If you can figure this out, then you have mastered the art of staging and can get closer to the results I'm about to share with you.

How HGTV Changed the Game

Research published by the National Association of Realtors shows that home buyers are willing to increase their offer price for an effectively staged-home by one to five percent when compared to non-staged-homes. If you're selling a home worth $200,000, this is a $2,000 to $10,000 price difference. If you're selling a home worth $1,000,000 (that's a million), then that's a $10,000 to $50,000 difference.

This is why it's funny when I see homeowners debate the commission of a real estate agent. When you go without an agent, you might save three percent, but have to do all of the work yourself. You can stage your home and nearly cover the cost of a real estate agent.

The data shows that for a few select homes, they can actually command a price that is six to 10 percent higher than non-staged homes. That's jaw-dropping astounding. For a $200,000 home, we're talking about an extra $12,000 to $20,000. On a one-million-dollar home, we're talking about $60,000 to $100,000. That's crazy.

And I know it's easy to throw your hands up and say, "Whoa, whoa, whoa. Stop right there, Alex. There is no way a buyer can be that simple. There is no way that by putting some furniture in a home that we can sell our home for thousands of dollars more." But, you can. That's what the data shows, and I can back it up by my own personal experience. Buyers really are that simple. You're not just selling a home. You're selling a dream. Effective staging does a great job at selling that dream.

Staging a home is becoming a requirement for all homeowners that want to create the perfect experience and get their home sold. Traditionally, it has been a strategy only the luxury market uses. But it's becoming a requirement for all. That's because HGTV has changed the entire game and the way people look at homes. The channels have done an excellent job at educating people on the home buying and selling process, and at the same time, we have seen buyer's expectations shift.

Every single consumer now wants a perfectly ready, move-in, turn-key home. They want your home looking like it came from a magazine. They want it to look like it could be featured on HGTV. Home buyers want a home that matches their exact taste and preferences. You need to make sure through staging you have matched a buyer's expectations and sold the dream.

By staging your home, you increase its perceived value, and that's what allows it to sell for more. Remember, perception outweighs reality. What people think your home is worth is far more important than what your home is actually worth. The more you can do to increase its perceived value, the higher you're going to be able to sell your home for.

With that said, I want to talk about a few common strategies for staging your home and how to craft the perfect experience so you can sell your home for more. Then, I will shift to how you can keep your home staged while your house is on the market. Getting your home staged is usually the easy part. Keeping it staged? That's another story.

Borrowing a Common Strategy from the Retail Industry

For a second, I want you to close your eyes and think back to the last store you visited. Specifically, I want you to think about the moment before you walked into the store and the moments after you walked in. Now, try to describe that experience. What was it like? You probably don't think much about this, but the retail industry has. In fact, they have run experiment after experiment trying to optimize your first few seconds in the store. They know first-impressions matter, so they spent a lot of time figuring out what created the best impression so that you would buy more.

When you enter any store, you immediately enter into an open space. It's called the "No-Engage Decompression Zone". This space should be empty and void of any workers and products. Humans are being increasingly inundated with external information — from our phones, to sounds, to advertising and more. However, it turns out that our brains have changed little in the last 300,000 years. We still can't effectively process a ton of information.

Based on research done in the retail industry, they found that people have more memorable experience and buy more when they are given a decompression zone. This zone gives them time to adjust from the outside to the inside. It will subconsciously transport visitors from a distracted mindset to a calmer state, ready to embrace the shopping experience. It takes a lot for our brains to shift. We need time to adjust to the new sensory input. When we step into a store our lighting has changed. The temperature, sound, and smell are all different. A decompression zone allows us to make that shift.

So, if retailers realized the importance of the shift that needs to happen with buyers to create a good experience and get them to buy more, shouldn't we be using it in real estate? Unlike the retail industry, I don't have enough data points to make a statistically significant assertion that a decompression zone will benefit you in getting your home sold. Instead, my theory is based on inference, reasoning, and anecdotal evidence.

Based on human behavior and psychology, I believe it's just as important to create a decompression zone in your home if you want to improve the experience and increase the chance a potential buyer makes an offer on your home. Just like a store, as soon as a home buyer enters a home, they are greeted with new sensory input — new lighting, new smells, a different temperature and new sounds. We need to give home buyers a chance to adjust to these inputs. We need to give them time to subconsciously shift from a distracted mindset to a calmer state. This will ensure they take the time to tour your home and have a better experience.

So, how do we set about creating a decompression zone? What exactly does it look like in our home? In the retail industry, it's common for a decompression zone to be about 15ft to 20ft wide. The size of the zone is dependent on the size of the overall store and layout. Some retailers might have a decompression zone that is only 3ft wide, while others have a zone that is 20ft wide. Obviously a 20ft wide decompression zone in a home is impossible for most. For that reason, we like to see a decompression zone of about three to five feet.

This zone should be void of furniture, clutter, and personal items. It needs to be an empty space. Any and all physical objects should be removed from the area where the home buyer will enter. We can all agree that first impressions matter, and the first few moments a home buyer enters your home are some of the most critical. It will set the stage for the rest of the home tour. If upon entering, a home buyer is greeted with clutter and junk, they won't be able to escape the distracted mindset their brain is in. As a result, they will move through the home fast and take very little interest.

The most common violation I see when it comes to decompression zones are coats and shoes. This is a natural place to put these items, but they are inside your decompression zone and create a poor buying experience. When I say this zone needs to be void of everything, I mean it. I mean that it really needs to be void of any items whatsoever. The zone is not about having things organized or clean. It's about being empty. Even junk can be organized. There should not be a single item within three to five feet of the entry point. If there is, you need to remove it.

Saving Time When Staging

When it comes to staging your home, not all rooms are considered equal. There are certain rooms that have a large influence on a buyer's decision. You will want to focus your efforts on these rooms and spend less time on the rooms that won't make much of a difference.

There are really only three rooms that hold the most importance for crafting the perfect experience for home buyers. They are the living room, the master bedroom, and the kitchen. These are the rooms that you want to focus on the most when you're staging your home. Don't worry so much about less influential rooms, like the bathrooms or children's room, or basement.

The living room is the place people will congregate the most to relax and enjoy their home. So, it's important that you tell the right story in your living room. You want a home buyer to dream about their life in your living room. It should fit their lifestyle. Go back to your target market and think about the lifestyle they want to live. Chances are that you are part of this market and you have the needed furniture to communicate this lifestyle.

For example, if your home is perfect for a growing family, then you want to make sure the living room fits a lifestyle that a growing family lives. You will likely want furniture, a TV, and an area for kids to play while the parents are in the living room. It should be a place for parents and kids to interact while providing relaxation to parents.

The second room you want to focus on is the master bedroom. You want this place to be an oasis. But what it looks like should match your market. An oasis is going to look very different for a married-family than a single 30-year-old bachelor. We all have stress and chaos in our life. No matter who you're designing you master bedroom for, it needs to be a place that people can go to and relax. They need to be able to imagine that after a long-stressful day, this is the place they can go to escape it all and refresh themselves.

The third room that you want to look at is the kitchen. Ideally, you will create enough space in the cabinets and cupboards that it appears to be functional. That means your cabinets and drawers should not be more than 75 percent full. Less is better of course. There is the old saying that the kitchen sells the home. For the most part, this is true. If you're stressed on time and don't plan to do any staging aside from one room, I recommend the kitchen.

But, if you focus on just these three rooms, you get will the biggest results. You don't need to stress about the whole home. These rooms will get the home sold for the least amount of effort. They will have the largest impact on the home buyer's experience. If we can stage these homes, and tell the right story, we can increase your home's perceived value — allowing us to sell more for your home than we could if it wasn't staged.

Disregard the Small Details And Buyers Will Pass

Home buyers can be a little unforgiving and picky. If you disregard the small details, it's more than likely a home buyer will pass on your home. And I really mean the smallest of details. I'm talking about the smallest particle of dust on your stove or the razor that was left on the bathroom sink. We need to make sure that even the small details are taken care of.

First, get rid of any clutter. The most basic task when staging a home involves removing clutter and cleaning the house. Remove the knick-knacks and personal items from all surfaces. Don't just put them in the closet. Big trucks, big homes, and big yards. We love our space. It's one of the reasons a lot of people want to buy a home. Add space to your home by getting all of the clutter out of the home. It's best to box it up and store it somewhere else.

Your closets and drawers should be less than 75% full. Anything beyond 75% is too crowded. It won't allow buyers to see that there is adequate storage space in the home. Over 55% of homeowners say that storage is important when buying a home. Only 35% are happy with their current home's storage capabilities.

If closets and drawers are jammed, buyers won't get a good sense for how much storage space is available. Storage is so important that appraisers count a room as a bedroom if it has an adequate closet. They don't look for proper fire escape or if it stores a bed. They look for a closet. If you need to get your space opened, consider donating some stuff, putting it in a storage unit or store it at a family member's house.

Second, with all of the clutter gone, do a deep cleaning. Make every square-inch sparkle, especially the kitchen. Small detail, but make sure your toilet lid is closed when people are touring the homes. These are the small details that I'm talking about which can kill the chance of your home selling.

Third, depersonalize your home. That means you need to make it look less like you live there so a home buyer can imagine themselves living there. Take down all of the photos of your family and any other personal items. If you leave these personal items out, people are going to feel like they are invading your home. That makes them uncomfortable and doesn't put them in a home buying experience. It's really tough to imagine yourselves living there when you feel like you're invading at home. Depersonalizing your home is a good idea from a safety standpoint, too. It's better that your buyers don't know about your family. You never know who is walking into your home.

You might wonder what you can do to improve your home experience through staging. Here's my recommendation. Go out for a nice dinner. Have some fun. When you come back, I want you to try to visit your home like a home buyer would. Put yourself in a buyer's mind. Get rid of any preconceived notions you have about how great your home is or the amount of work you put into it. All of that is going to be irrelevant to a potential home buyer.

Your goal is to look at your home with fresh eyes. Look at everything. When you first drive up to your home, look at it from both angles. Drive by the home both ways. Over time, we become blind to any issues with our home. For example, I remember one home seller I spoke with had become blind to the weeds in his driveway. At first, his driveway was perfectly clear. But weeds started to grow. They were small at first until they became giant clusters of weeds. He had become blind to it and hadn't realized that this might distract a home buyer. Honestly, he didn't even notice it until I pointed it out.

You have to come to your home with fresh eyes. Everything in your home didn't happen overnight. It was the result of years. If you have trouble looking at your home with fresh eyes, consider asking the opinion of a real estate agent. They can give you an unbiased opinion on how to stage your home to craft the perfect experience.

How to Maintain a Staged Home

Great, you've finally decluttered and depersonalized everything in your home. You have created a home that tells the perfect story for your market. It's going to create a top-notch experience. Now comes the hard part... how do you maintain a staged home and keep your home in constant show-ready condition? Note: this section is relevant even if you don't plan to live in the home while you're selling it.

One of the biggest mistakes I see with vacant homes is homeowners not check in on their homes enough. I can't tell you the number of homes I have been to that were vacant in the middle of Winter, so they had a lot of dried salt-water on their floors. If your home will be vacant, be sure to check on it in between showings. If you will be living in the home, especially with kids, then you have some unique challenges. How do you keep a home clean when it seems like the only objective of a toddler is to make everything a mess and bring chaos?

When it comes to maintaining a staged home, it's best to be proactive. Creating your own checklists and schedules, then delegating some of the chores to family members is a great way to get started. It's in the small daily habits and how you initially declutter your home that will determine how hard or easy it is to keep your home in show-ready condition. For example, if you decluttered, then there shouldn't be a ton of items you need to reorganize or put away every day. A small new habit that makes sure every item goes back into the drawer when you're done with it is an easy way to prevent chores from piling up and having to be taken care of moments before showing. Here are some tips to follow to keep your home staged.

The first piece of advice I have for you is to plan your week. Not everything in your home will need to be cleaned on a daily basis or moments before showing. For example, you can designate Mondays to cleaning your hardwood floors. It's unlikely you need to clean every single day. Of course, if you're showing your home in the winter, you may need to clean it a bit more often. Other items, like your kitchen tile, may not need to be cleaned more than once a week. It's important to keep these things on a regular schedule so that you can keep them clean.

Second, create a new designated place for stuff that enters your home, or better yet, take care of it the moment you get it. It's easy to throw junk mail on the table or to shove your key somewhere at the end of the day. You need to get out of the habit of tossing items on a table or the ground and leaving them there to build clutter. Especially when it comes to your entryway. We want the entryway to be clear. This is your decompression zone and it should be clear of any items. Your mail, keys, jackets, and shoes need to find another place to go.

My third tip, make sure you're staying on top of your landscaping on at least a weekly basis. You may need to this on a daily basis or may get away with doing it on an as needed basis. For example, in the winter, you may need to go out after every snowfall to remove any snow from your walkways and to put down some salt. In the summer, you may need to cut your grass on a weekly basis. During the fall, there may be little landscaping you have to do aside from picking up some leaves when they fall. You want to make sure your home and curb appeal are stunning. Real estate agents and home buyers need to be able to easily access your home. Remember, inability to access the front door or the key box can create a bad experience and we don't want that to happen.

Fourth, before you go to work every day, I recommend that you take about 10 minutes and remove items that don't belong on countertops, table tops, and vanities. If possible, take a rag and quickly clean these services and sweep up any messes that

HOW TO SELL ANY HOME... EVEN THE HARD TO SELL HOMES

might have occurred during dinner or breakfast. You never know when a showing request is going to come in. By having your home ready, you won't have to rush home after work to get the place cleaned up. You can take your time and rest easy knowing that your home is already show ready, so if someone requests a showing for the evening on the same day, you can make it happen.

Fifth tip, I want you to try to do some light dusting and vacuuming on a daily basis. If you live a busy and active lifestyle, consider investing in a robotic vacuum to take care of the mess while you're away at work. That way if a buyer calls and needs to see your home in the evening, it won't be mad dash to get home and clean. Also, you will want to make sure to clean the dishes on a daily basis, even if you had a dishwasher. People will open up your dishwasher and they do not want to see dirty dishes. You should also make sure your garbage is cleaned out for every showing. It's best to do these on a daily basis so they don't pile up for the weekend. Otherwise, you will have a very busy weekend.

On a daily basis, you will also want to make your beds. You can instantly make a bedroom look put together when you make the bed. Sloppy beds are a bad experience. Make the beds. You will also want to quickly clean the bathroom on a daily basis. In the morning, wipe down the shower and all surfaces to remove any mildew and to prevent any water stains. If possible, have some clean white towels available and make sure the family doesn't use them. This will give your bathroom an overall clean look and feel. Think like a hotel experience.

Last tip. Keep the laundry constantly moving throughout the home. Clean clothes as soon as you have enough to do a load. Your clothes should not be stored until the weekend. Clothes should never be left on the floor and should be placed, instead, in a hamper that is hidden and hides the clothes. Keep them out of site. It's better to have the clothes cleaned and kept in drawers or closets.

I know it sounds like a pain to do all of this on a daily basis, but we're talking about thousands of extra dollars in earnings when your home sells. You can do these and sell your home for more money because you created the perfect experience, or you can neglect these and sell your home for less (or risk it sitting on the market). If you take some of these tasks and give them to the whole family, it makes it a little bit easier. It's important to understand that these crucial tasks and these small details can make or break the sale of your home. I know the struggle will be real and there'll be a lot of days that you're going to get angry because your house hasn't sold it. But remember that the situation is not permanent. It's only until your house sells. And your efforts will be well worth it.

ONE THING

By staging your home and telling the perfect story, get more real estate agents and home buyers to buy your home.

4 M IS FOR MARKETING (PART 1): BUILDING THE PERFECT PROFILE

Now that we've talked about the experience of your home, I want to shift our focus into the marketing aspect of our TEAM formula. If you hire a real estate agent, this is the element they will be most responsible for. They will be investing their money upfront — with the risk of no return — in an effort to get your home sold.

So, while the average homeowner doesn't need to have these skills, it's important to understand and learn the tips and strategies I'm about to go over. They will help you find a real estate agent. Everything I share with you will give you a scorecard for evaluating your real estate agent. You can see what makes a perfect listing profile and if your real estate agent has built a profile that will get results.

When it comes to marketing, there are two categories we use to break up our marketing strategy; our listing profile and the promotion of the home. In other words, how does your home look on sites like Zillow, the Multiple-Listing Service, and Realtor.com? Then, how are we getting home buyers to view your profile? The goal of your listing profile is to generate interest and ideally a conversion (defined as a lead captured or a home buyer taking a tour of your home). The goal of promotion is to let every single homeowner know that your home is for sale. We can often measure it by the total views or traffic to your listing profile or the number of people saving your home in their search results.

In this chapter, we are going to dive deeper into the perfect listing profile. Then, in a later chapter, we will cover the promotional side of marketing. So, let's get started on how to create the best listing profile that turns web site visitors to Zillow into home buyers who tour your home.

How Buyers Decide Which Homes to Preview

To understand how to build our listing profile, it helps by understanding how buyers decide which homes to preview. How does a buyer go from a web visitor on Zillow to asking their agent to tour a specific home? For a second, I want you to imagine that you're a home buyer. If you're in the market to buy a home, then this shouldn't be hard for you to imagine. You can think about your own experience and behavior when house hunting.

First, a home buyer visits a site like Zillow. They search for all of the homes in their city, with little search parameters. For example, they will type in "Lansing, MI" and get all of the homes for sale in Lansing. At any given time, there might be 2,000+ listings in my area. With 2,000+ listings to look through, how does a home buyer decide which ones to click? You would like to wish that home buyers have a budget, they would search for homes within that budget, and then they would give equal attention to all of the homes that match their criteria. That's just not what happens.

Thanks to the internet, buyers have access to thousands of homes at their fingertips. Combine that with a home buyer's fears of missing out on the perfect home, and you have a home buyer who would rather search through 2,000+ listings for the sake of "finding something that could be a good fit for them." But all of this information has a cost. It takes a lot of time to search through this many listings. Who can really make the time to research 2,000+ homes?

Instead, home buyers look for ways to filter out the information themselves. Rather than setting up search parameters, they use the main listing photo to determine whether they click or not. Every home buyer searches like this. They're sitting at the Doctor's office or waiting for their kids to get out school, thumbing through thousands of listings on Zillow, and only stopping at the ones they really love. They click on the ones that grab their attention and pull them. All of this means that you have one shot (pun intended) to virtually grab a potential buyer by their shirt and pull them in. One shot to connect with them and stand out from all of the other listings.

My question to you is this. How do you stand out from the thousands of listings that a home buyer is sifting through? If you can't stand out, you risk drowning in the sea of thousands of listings. A great listing photo is what will grab a buyers attention. It will get them to click on your profile. Once you have their attention on your profile, you will use the rest of the photos and listing description to get a home buyer to turn into a buyer who tours your home.

To determine if your home is worth seeing, a buyer will look at the rest of your photos. They will try to imagine themselves living there. They will then read the listing description and small details, like the square footage and lot size. They will make sure these match what they are looking for. Lastly, they will often compare your asking price to the automated value estimate. On Zillow, this is called the Zestimate. A Zestimate that is too far off may scare plenty of home buyers.

Building a great listing profile is the difference between home buyers deciding to preview your home or skipping it. A poor listing profile will result in poor showing results, even if your marketing is top-notch. A great profile can sometimes survive poor marketing and result in a high number of showings. Needless to say, building a great listing profile forms the base of your marketing. A good listing profile aided by a great promotional plan will get you the highest number of showings.

I'm not suggesting it's a perfect solution and you will win every time, but you will certainly win more times than not.

Selling An Investment Property

"Alex Craig is a pleasure to work with! He is organized, conscientious, and we feel like we made a friend after working with him. Such a hard worker! He was willing to go to great lengths to help us sell our house. We can't say enough good things about him! The next time we need the services of a real estate agent, Alex will be the only one we'll call. We will be sure to recommend him to family and friends!"

-Sue Goodenow; Lansing, MI

SUCCESS STORY QUICK WINS

Meet Sue and Charles: After their once perfect rental home turned into a negative cash flow investment, Sue and Charles decided it was time to sell their home. They were ready to move on.

How We Helped Them Sell Their Home: We helped Sue

and Charles navigate the issues that come with trying to sell a home while there is a tenant occupying the property. We also launched a highly-targeted marketing campaign that went after Lansing real estate investors.

Results: It worked. We were able to get Sue and Charles out of their investment property so they could focus on living their life and not worrying about a cash flow negative investment.

If you're a real estate investor, you know a perfect investment property can become a bad rental. This usually happens when you need to restructure your financing, forgot to account for capital expenditures like the roof, or find out you've been charging too low of rent. Suddenly, the property that was a healthy cash cow is sick. It's costing money from your own pocket every single month to have a tenant in your rental.

That was the case for my clients Sue and Charles. In the late 1990's, they purchased a home on Clyde and turned it into a rental property. For many years the property produced a positive cash flow for them. They took money to the bank every month.

But at some point, their healthy cow became sick and became a cash eating monster. There were several reasons for this, but the two main reasons were refinancing and when the market crashed in 2008. It caused them to pay out more than they were receiving. With the rental home costing them every single month — in terms of money and headaches. They knew it was time to sell the home. The market was doing well, so they wanted to get rid of it.

How Do You Deal With Tenants When Selling?

Selling a home with a tenant can be a challenge. As a homeowner, you typically have opposite goals than your tenant. Your goal is to sell your home. Your tenant doesn't care if you sell. In fact, your tenant may wish that your home doesn't sell so they can still live in the home. Unless a potential buyer is an investor, hardly anyone wants to purchase a home with a tenant in it.

For that reason, every situation with a tenant needs to be evaluated. You have to answer questions like, "Is it better to sell your home with the tenant living there or should you wait until their lease agreement ends? Do you let the tenant move out and possibly face negative cash flow until the house sells?"

In our situation, we decided it was better to give the renter a bonus if he cooperated with showings and kept the place clean for showings. Since the tenant was on month-to-month lease, we decided to give the tenant 60 days to vacate the property. We figured it would be better to take a more negative cash flow position to get the home sold and be done with it. This way, Sue and Charles could move on.

Marketing To Real Estate Investors

After evaluating potential target markets, I decided it would be best to appeal to Lansing real estate investors. The home needed some repairs and was in an ideal rental neighborhood. So, that's what I did. I put together a marketing plan that tightly targeted real estate investors in Lansing. "Such a hard worker! [Alex] was willing to go to great lengths to help us sell our house," said Sue.

And Sue is right. I went to great lengths to get the home sold. First, our plan started with creating a solid listing profile built around professional real estate photos and a listing description. Second, we took our listing profile and launched Facebook ads targeting real estate investors. Now, on Facebook you can't directly target real estate investors. There isn't a category for real estate investors. Instead, we need to find parallel interests that indicate a user may be a real estate investor. In our case, we targeted people who had in interest in sites like Bigger Pockets, Fortune Builders, and Dean Graziosi, an author who wrote books on real estate investing.

We had some decent results in terms of interest and clicks on Facebook. We got 261 link clicks for around $73. We got the house in front of 5,528 people. In addition to our ads, we directly reached out to all of the real estate investors we had in our database and customer relationship management software.

This is what sold the home… connections are important. It's important to work with a real estate agent who can tap into their own database and leads to get your home sold. Most real estate agents list a home and then try to generate a buyer. For several homes, we often have buyer leads we can market your home to. One of the real estate investors we reached out to, who is also a Lansing real estate agent, made an offer on the property. And Sue and Charles were happy about this deal.

Not Every Deal Ends Cash Positive

No matter how I structured the offer, my client would need to bring money to the closing table. However, what I could do is minimize the amount they would have to bring. And that's what I did. I was able to get them a fair price offer for the home and save on selling costs since the buyer was a real estate agent. This meant they didn't need to pay the buyer's commission because he could waive it.

> At the end of the day, my seller was able to pay a smaller amount than if we waited out for an offer from another investor. While it may not end cash positive, it is possible for EVERY deal to end positive. "Alex Craig is a pleasure to work with! He is organized, conscientious, and we feel like we made a friend after working with him," said Sue. He was willing to go to great lengths to help us sell our house. We can't say enough good things about him! The next time we need the services of a real estate agent, Alex will be the only one we'll call. We will be sure to recommend him to family and friends! She didn't make money, but she made a friend. And I made a friend. Sue and Charles are one of Dolinski Group's favorite clients and we will be around to help them in all of their real estate needs.

How To Build A Great Listing Profile

Your listing profile is the foundation to your marketing. It needs to be solid, otherwise your other marketing efforts won't matter much. Building a week listing profile is kind of like building a house on sand. The moment the first storm arrives, the home will wash away. To build the best listing profile, there are three core elements — your photos, your listing description, and how close the asking price is to the Zestimate. We will also look at whether it's worth adding video tours or 3D tours to your listing profiles.

When it comes to your photos, this is the core element that will cause visitors to click on your profile. So, it stands to reason that your photos are critical to getting your home sold. I see a lot of people shoot photos with their phone. While phones have become powerful cameras, they should not substitute the work of a professional real estate photographer. A real estate photographer has a skill set and knowledge that goes beyond the quality of the photo. They understand how to create memorable images, and they know how to tell the right story with these

HOW TO SELL ANY HOME... EVEN THE HARD TO SELL HOMES

photos. Great photos are about taking the right angles, having the right balance, and more.

Your listing description and "Zestimate" will be what converts a potential buyer looking on your profile to someone that requests a showing. The biggest mistake I see when it comes to the listing description is selling the features of the home. This is the highest-level that you can sell on. We believe selling happens on three levels. There is your feature level, which describes what you get. Then, there is the benefits level, which describes the benefits you can expect from these features. Then, there is the outcome or the result, which are all about selling the dream. Most listing descriptions focus on the feature level, and this the weakest level of selling. In this chapter, we will cover how to write powerful listing descriptions that get results.

Photos: How Many Are Necessary?

One photo will create the majority of your results. One photo will be responsible for all of the clicks you get to your profile. Does that mean you should have only one quality photo and the rest don't matter? To answer that, we have to look at the purpose of Zillow and how they generate revenue. At the end of the day, Zillow has a responsibility to its shareholders, investors, and real estate agents.

Zillow's revenue model is simple. They make money by selling advertising space to real estate agents. Real estate agents give Zillow money in an effort to gain market exposure and generate home buyer leads. So, if home buyers go, then real estate agents will follow suit, and Zillow's entire revenue stream will dry up. This means, Zillow needs to focus on driving traffic to their website and then keeping that traffic there long enough for them to submit a form. One of the best ways to do this is by focusing on the quality of the user experience (from the home buyer's perspective).

Zillow can keep their user experience high by showing homes that are, first, relevant, and second, complete. Meaning, two homes in the same neighborhood, within the same budget preferences, number of bedrooms and the number of bathrooms will be ranked by the best profile — most photos, detailed information, and pricing. More photos become a way to get your home ranked in Zillow's search engine. It allows you to beat out your competition. They won't guarantee a ranking, but they improve your odds.

While Zillow hasn't come out to say that photo quantity doesn't influence the ranking in the search results of Zillow, there seems to be correlation. Based on our research through hundreds of search results across the Lansing, MI area, there seems to be a correlation that says the more photos, the higher the results. We've found the median number of the first home to be around 40 photos. Buyer don't need 40 photos, but that's what it takes to increase your odds of beating the competition.

I see plenty of homes, that hope to sell, with only 10 photos. That's too few. The only way to produce better results than the average is to do more than the average. This means you need as many photos as you can get and upload them to your listing profile.

Often, I see some homes only take five exterior photos because the inside isn't in the best condition. Real estate agents use this strategy to entice home buyers. They figure, if there is enough intrigue that maybe a home buyer will schedule a showing. Not true.

This strategy will actually backfire on you. The new economy doesn't have any patience for those kinds of tactics. If you try to play that game, you will lose. There isn't a doubt about that. Buyers demand to see everything about your home before they check it out. Failure to do otherwise means they will hit the back button and look for homes that do have complete pictures.

It comes down to only two elements; your pictures and your listing description. Among buyers who used the internet during their home search process, 89% of them found photos very useful and 85% found detailed information about the home for sale very useful. When we look at other studies like those published in the Wall Street Journal we see "listings with nicer photos gain anywhere between $935 and $116,076 more than those that neglect to implement the necessary techniques and technology."

Yeah that's a huge difference but tons of studies show that buyers want to see photos of a home and that they help sell the home. That means everything else on your Zillow profile is only going to make a margin difference that might not be worth it. Of course, as a realtor, I try to optimize all of it for my clients but you might not need to. For example, the Zestimate has been linked to influencing buyer perception but it's only marginal compared to photos. Focusing on the 20% is a great way to optimize for your efforts but if want to optimize for quality, then you will need to focus on all 100%.

Capturing Memorable Images

Photography is certainly an art, but it can be boiled down into a science, too. This helps everyone take quality photos that attract home buyers. The best thing you can do to get your home sold, if you haven't done so already, is get quality photography taken. Here's some of the Dos and Don'ts or real estate photography.

DO — take your picture from the curb. It's best if you can stand across the street or in the street. You're looking to capture your entire home and show off that curb appeal. While the traditional driving around and looking at homes isn't as common anymore, people still want to see that in a photo.

The photo should look like it came from someone who is driving by. So, place your camera (or tripod) about 4 feet high. That's the approximate height of people sitting in a car. Stay that height unless you're trying to do aerial photos. If your house is taller, you will want to angle the camera up to capture the home.

DON'T — keep around any distracting items. I have to shake my head every time that I see someone take photos and they leave their cars in the driveway. First, the car usually covers some feature of the garage or the home, so people don't really even get to see what your home is like. Second, it's hard for buyers to imagine living in a home when your car is parked in the driveway. Third, I have security issues with it. I suppose it's fine, but people can run your plates and find out who you are. I know plates are all over but to me, it's opening yourself up to some level of risk.

DO — try to make your door the focal point. This is psychological trick that I use and have photographers use. It's so subtle and most people don't notice it, but it makes a world of difference. By making the door the focal point, you're welcoming buyers to take a look at the rest of your photos. You are setting the tone for the rest of your home.

Robert Cialdini in his book The Psychology of Persuasion he talks about small commitments in an effort to continue to persuade people. Using the door as a focal point is asking buyers for a small commitment. You're asking them to come look at your Zillow profile and click on it. Once they click on it, you will have other commitments, like get them to come see the home. Then, get them to make an offer.

DO — consider using aerial photos for expensive homes, larger homes or homes that have unique features. An example is a home that has a lot of land, a horse barn, and maybe some trails on the property. Plus, according to the MLS homes with aerial photos tend to sell 68% faster than homes without aerial photography. Aerial photography is a great way to capture all of the features of a home and sell a lifestyle not just a home. Buying is an emotional experience and hardly any of us by a home for functional use. We buy it because what the home has to offer.

Aerial photos also tend to standout in Zillow. Not every seller does it so that's a huge bonus. It hasn't it what famous startup consultant, Andrew Chen, calls the "law of shitty click throughs". That when we discover a method that works, eventually a lot of people start to discover it and the results begin to suffer because of the competition.

Andrew states that over time all marketing strategies result in shitty clickthrough. It works, then it doesn't. As realtors discover a strategy that works more realtors will start to use it and over time it will get less results. A simple example is the banner ad. If you remember when banner ads started, they had click through rates of 75%. Meaning, for every 100 people that saw the banner, 750 people would click on it. Now, forget it. You have a better chance at becoming a Navy Seal than clicking on a banner ad. But for now, I think there are few more months or years left on aerial photography in our area. You can expect to enjoy it and get good results until 2019 or later. By then, us realtors will think of something else.

DO — take advantage of the seasons and update your photos. One mistake I see from realtors is that a house that doesn't sell well and sits on the market will start to show its age with out of season photos. I recently ran across a photo of a new construction home that had photos with snow on the ground and the roof. It's only a light blanket. Maybe an inch. The problem? Well, if it's summer, people will be able to instantly see that this house has been sitting on the market for a very, very long time.

It's a good idea to update your photos so that people don't see that your home has been sitting on the market long. If it seems like it's been on the market a long time, buyers will question what the heck is wrong with your home. Updating your photos can make an old listing look new and give it some life to generate new leads.

DO — try to capture what's called the dawn shot. This is challenging to pull off and isn't for the faint of heart. It requires you to be really good at timing. When the sun is nearly setting, turn all of the lights on in your house. This will create a beautiful contrast that will make your home shine. If you do this, I recommend hiring an expert unless you're really good at photography yourself.

DON'T — neglect your lines. Our brains are wired with a built-in ruler. We love when lines are leveled. Think about your natural preference for a photo on the wall… does it bother you when the photo's frame isn't perfectly leveled and aligned with the floor? It bothers me. And that's because as humans, we feel uncomfortable and odd when things are visually unbalanced. Our subconscious has the ability to feel when something is off.

Why is your TV properly aligned on a wall? Why are your photos perfectly aligned with the floor? Why does your computer sit on a flat surface? Crooked lines don't feel natural and they're difficult to look at. It's impossible for us to stare at a photo on the wall that's crooked. It's the same with when buyers are looking through search results on sites like Zillow.

To create a sense of stability and calmness, we have to find the horizontal line in our photos and make sure it's parallel to the photo's frame. Your horizontal line is likely going to be the roof or the surface horizon. Next, just tilt the photo in a photo editor until the horizon is parallel with the photo's frame.

DON'T — leave your photos unedited. Most of the time, your camera won't capture the right colors and feeling. You will need to draw contrast between different features of the home and things like that. You might want the grass to look greener. The best tool is photoshop, which if you haven't you can download for a free trial while your home is for sale. But you can also use things like Pixlr Editor to get those elements to really pop.

You Got Them to View Your Listing: How to Keep Them and Convert Them

Many real estate agents look at the listing description as useless and optional. It cracks me up to see some of the listing descriptions (or lack thereof really) that people post. It's funny because as buyers, we want every single piece of information but when we go to sell our own home, we do the exact opposite of how people buy. Instead, we say that it doesn't matter. But personal experience, watching hundreds of buyers, and the data shows otherwise. People care about your listing description.

Why do some agents and owners expect buyers to behave differently than we do? The truth is that they're not. This new economy is incredibly tough on a home seller. You have to disclose everything if you want a buyer to even come look at your home. There are far too many lazy listing descriptions on Zillow.

HOW TO SELL ANY HOME... EVEN THE HARD TO SELL HOMES

So, this is one way to really stand out from the average agent and your competition. How many times have you seen a description like:

"3-bedroom, 2-bathroom home in Okemos with 2,000+ sqft of space."

That's it. All of that information is already included in the Zillow features of a home. And maybe deep down inside it's the copywriter in me that comes out and claws way out. But when I see a listing description like that, I just shake my head. Too many people undervalue the power of words. Few people have mastered the art of creating listing descriptions. They focus on features of the home like 3-bedrooms. In copywriting, we have a common mindset that says you should always focus on the benefits. Not the features. A feature says what a home has to offer while the benefit describes why it matters. Here are some examples:

- 4th bedroom — playroom for the kids so you don't have toys on the floor all over the house.
- Open kitchen layout — you can watch your kids while you cook.

Copy has the ability to invoke emotion in a way that images don't. Plus, they add to the photos. Someone might be able to see the hardwood floors in the photo, but they can't appreciate them until you tell them the wood type and why that's a good thing. They might see the two-car garage but describe to them what could fit into the garage. I always say that photos will get the clicks, but words will get the phone calls. If you want people to actually call for a tour, you need to get a lot better at writing a listing description.

Writing Your Listing Description

To write your listing description, determine the features of your home that home buyers are sure to love. Ask yourself, "what do buyers want?" Not all buyers are created equal. It's important to target the home buyer's you believe are most likely to buy your home. You will need to be careful violating any kind of Fair Housing Laws, so do watch out for words like "kids" or "family". Once you have an idea of what buyers are looking for, look around your neighborhood and see what else is on the market.

Let's say you have a one-story single-family home and all of the homes in your neighborhood bi-level. This could be a huge selling point for someone looking to downsize and live in that neighborhood. It's unique. It wouldn't be unique if every home around was also single story.

For a starting point, here are some features that might be unique:

- Location — could be a certain neighborhood, subdivision, school district, or proximity to an important landmark or employer.
- Views — Anything like nature and lakes will attract people and are unique.
- Privacy — many people have dogs and kids. They like to have a fence and a private fence. Privacy is important. This is one of the reasons people chose a home over an apartment.
- Layout — open house floor plans are all the rage right now. Thanks to HGTV. But it could also include layouts like ranch styles for people looking to downsize.

Let's say that your home has a fenced in backyard but a majority of the homes in the neighborhood don't have a fence. That's a unique feature and you should let people know about it. A picture could tell me that you have the backyard but it's only the description that will tell me which features are unique. It's why I say that descriptions sell. Do you have a deck overlooking the Grand River? Include it. Highlight it both in your photos but also describe the unique view. How many houses are available that overlook the Grand River?

Just remember that the feature needs to be unique when compared to the homes that your potential buyers might be looking at. So, you will want to look at other homes in your neighborhood that are for sale. Do you have something that those houses don't? You will also want to compare your home to those that are in different neighborhoods but are around the same price point and have similar bedrooms, bathrooms, and square footage. So, once you have your features, let's look at how to turn it into beautiful copy that get buyer practically begging to see your home.

Step #1: Write down what they're going to "get" when they buy your home. This is simply the features that we discovered earlier. This is a pretty easy part once you spend some time doing research. While it's easy, you have to understand that 80% of the work is done upfront. Abraham Lincoln said "give me an hour to chop down a tree and I will spend most of it sharpening my ax" [look this up]. This means, that you need to get the right features first.

For an example, a buyer will get a (1) two-car garage, (2) 2,500 square feet of living, and (3) a fireplace. It's that straightforward. We're not focused on trying to dress and embellish our copy. In fact, don't do that. We're starting with what I call a plain English description. There are no tricks, the copy is plain that anybody can understand it. The next steps will explore how to improve on this.

Step #2: Paint a picture. Next, we're going to describe what the prospect could do with the feature of a home. We want to tell them the significance of this feature and paint a picture for them. People are incredibly terrible at imaging themselves in your home, so we have to tell them what it would be like.

Let's walks through an example with the fireplace feature from above. To paint a picture, I might say something like:

"Sit by the fireplace with your blanket and book."

That's a good start and is probably fine to move to the next step for most of us. Very few realtors know how to write effective copy. I like to say that a one-eyed man can lead in the land of the blind. Meaning, you can dominate with mediocre copy because everyone else produces terrible copy. But for this, I want to take it a step further to give you an idea of what's possible and to show you how to really create irresistible copy. I always think it's worth spending the extra few minutes. We're already sitting and writing this. Remember that ordinary actions will get ordinary results. So, let's expand this:

"When it's freezing outside, snuggle up to your warm and cozy fireplace with a good book."

Alright, now we're talking. There is a lot of copy in the description that I want to dissect. The first, and probably most important, is the word "your". The single most powerful word in copywriting is you. It gets people to imagine this fireplace as theirs. And people are always thinking about themselves. Once we have a good description, we're going to make it even better by adding vivid and specific details.

Step #3: Add vivid and specific detail. Here we want to add details that allows a potential buyer to experience your home with as many of their senses as possible. The senses are touch, taste, smell, hear, and sight. You're mostly going to use touch and sight through the use of colors, size, and other details. At this stage, I'm going to expand the fireplace example to something like:

"When it's a cold and snowy Michigan winter, let the warmth from the white-painted brick fireplace rest on your skin while you snuggle up with your grandma's handmade quilt, a cup of hot chocolate, and a copy of James Patterson's latest Mystery Novel."

There is no right or wrong answer to this, and you don't have to write how I do. This is where creativity comes in and you can express your character or try to talk to a specific market. For example, I could have written the copy like this:

"The crackling of the dry wood in your white-painted brick fireplace can be a soothing noise as you watch the Santa Clarita Diet and have a 'Netflix and Chill' kind of night."

Still great copy and follows all of the rules I laid out, but very different. Sure, it's a bit shorter and doesn't include as many details as the first one but it still has a lot of character and uses the senses. Quick note on how to stay out of trouble with Fair Housing Laws. The biggest mistake I see is people write something like, "perfect for families." My rule of thumb: never say something is perfect for someone. Notice in the fireplace example I didn't say the fireplace was perfect for anybody. In fact, I never said perfect. It drops the quality of your copy anyways because as buyers, we know stuff is rarely perfect.

I see a lot of realtors say things like, "this fireplace is perfect for the person that loves to sit by fires." Seriously, avoid that stuff in your copy. It's what I refer to as flowery or bombastic words. They fill their copy with words that sound good and fancy but don't really add any value to the copy. They're often words that are over exaggerations. It makes a listing description comes across as salesy and inauthentic. It makes you seem like the used car salesman.

Aside from words like perfect, other examples include: Anything that ends in -est. Examples include friendliest, greatest, best, coziest, and quietest. Buyers are cynical to these words as they're often over used. First, very homes are number 1 in what they have. Second, the words are subjective. Your definition of quietest is totally different than mine. I live with a ton of mini humans (children). My definition of quiet is probably pretty loud.

Words that have zero meaning. These are words like state-of-the-art and updated. They are devoid of meaning. They demand effort from the reader without any reward. It makes the copy ugly and nonsensical.

Avoid using words like really and very. Rather than very beautiful, why not say stunning? Rather than really nice fireplace, why not say a fantastic fireplace?

Unless your home really is number one in something, avoid words that imply it is. Instead, we want to use specific examples. If you look at the fireplace description, I didn't describe it as being the greatest in anything. I talked about it being a "white-painted brick" fireplace.

The second advice is to skip adjectives when they don't change the meaning of a sentence. This is often the case for a lot of listing descriptions I read. These are often in the form of adjectives like nice, beautiful, state of the art, updated, and more. We want to add specific details. Compare a traditional description that you might see:

"The kitchen includes beautiful and glossy cherry cabinets."

Vs.

"Cherry cabinets hang on the west side of the kitchen wall. They're made of a sturdy 18mm board, better than anything you can get at IKEA, and is polished with a scratch-resistant finish that is sure to keep your cabinets looking good for years to come."

See the difference? The first one just takes up space. It doesn't really add any value. I mean, what does beautiful mean? If I hate cherry cabinets, then they're not beautiful to me. But by focusing on specific details that are objective and facts, it's impossible to argue with it. I can't argue with the fact that the cabinets are 18mm thick or that it has a scratch-resistant finish.

Make an Offer They Can't Refuse

If a potential buyer has gotten all the way to the bottom, then they're interested in your home. Sometimes, no matter how good your copy, it won't get people to call you and they need a little extra nudge to pick up the phone now. When it comes to buying a home, there are a ton of reasons to wait. Buyers don't want to make a mistake so they often move slow and don't go see homes that might be a good fit for them.

To overcome this tendency to wait until later, you can use special offers. Since you're not using an agent, you can afford to make a special offer that will get people to call you and get your home sold faster. Now, this part isn't necessary and it's 100% optional. Depending on how desirable your home is and the market, you might not even need it. But when selling is tough, having a special offer goes a long way in getting your home sold faster.

An offer can come in many forms, but it's composed of two basic elements: an incentive that a potential buyer is likely to care about and a time limit. Let's explore each in a bit more detail.

Your incentive could be anything that you think a buyer might want, but common incentives are to offer seller's concession, which means you pay for closing costs. This is valuable to buyers who don't have a lot of money. It's often geared towards first-time home buyers. You could also offer to pay for the inspection or even to split the commission difference. For example, if you're saving 3% on a home, you might give the buyer 1% of that.

Another offer could be a home warranty. Personally, I don't think an owner should ever sell a home alone without a home warranty — no matter the market. A home warranty is a one-year protection plan to cover major appliances and systems so that buyers can have peace of mind when they take possession of the home. A home warranty will cover the repair or replace costs for appliances and systems like:

- Heating and cooling
- Internal plumbing
- Internal electrical
- Major appliances if sold with the home

- Septic systems

The total cost of a warranty is usually about $300 to $400 for a basic plan and as high as $600 for a comprehensive plan. In a seller's market, buyers don't really care about home warranties because they are competing with many buyers for few homes. They will take it as long as they love it. Since they don't really care, many people believe it's just a waste of money.

Personally, if you're selling alone, you should always sell with a home warranty because it can be absorbed into the cost of the house. So, in reality, it doesn't cost you anything. People will often pay a premium for peace of mind. If not, we wouldn't buy insurance like we do or take the extra warranty that is offered when we go buy a new car.

Let's say two homes are worth exactly $200,000. Yours has a $400 insurance policy on it and another one doesn't. You can get away with selling your home for $200,400. Just roll it into the cost. And because comparing homes like that is damn near difficult, nobody will be able to know whether or not they're actually paying for the cost of the home warranty. It's that simple.

Realtors will often do this to cover their commission. They will increase a home's sale price to cover the cost of their commission. They'll take a home's current sale price and divide it by 97% to get the value they would need to sell for to net you the same amount and still get their commission rate.

When you understand how home prices are actually determined, you will see that this commission rate is actually taken into account and the values of homes increase. For example, a home that is worth $200,000 will often sell for $206,000 and as a result all other homes will sell for that price.

A perfect example is seller's concessions which is often included in the sale price. So, if I offer $206,000 for your home that is $200,000 it will show that I'm paying $200,000 for your home and asking for $3,000 in concessions. But when we pull market data, it will show your home sold for $203,000. But the net on your home didn't change. Even though you got $3,000 more for the sale price, you had to pay $3,000 at the closing table.

Another common offer is actually not for the buyer, but for the realtor. This can be incredibly effective. Since nearly 90% of buyers use an agent, it's a good idea to offer an incentive to an agent. If you were able to bring a buyer without an agent, you would save 6% on your home's sale price. To bring a buyer, some owners will offer a buyer's commission of 3%. It's standard for buyer's and seller's agents to split commissions right down the middle, so owners will offer 3% but there is no rule that requires this.

Since the majority of homes will offer 3%, you can incentivize agents by offering 4% to a buyer's agent and you save 2%. A lot of agents will bring their buyers because they want that extra money. You could offer 4% for the first 30 days and 3.5% after that.

The second aspect of an offer is a timeline. Since the goal is to get a buyer to call you and not wait. It's a good idea to put a timeline on your offer. I recommend that you keep it under 30 days and do it within the first month of having your home listed. So, you might offer to cover seller's concessions during the first 30 days and after that, you won't. Or it could be something else.

There really is no limit to what you can offer as long as you're following Fair Housing Laws. For example, you could give a gift bag to people as a condition of touring your home. It doesn't have to be related to selling your home.

ONE THING

Build your listing profile. It will form the base of your marketing efforts.

5 M IS FOR MARKETING (PART 2): PROMOTING YOUR HOME FOR SALE

You've built a solid base with your listing profile, but all of it is useless if you can't start driving home buyer traffic to your profile. Sure, we can expect a certain level of traffic to come from Zillow. That's why we focused on optimizing our profile in the last chapter. However, we will need to drive more traffic to our profile. The homes that sell in ANY market are the ones with a solid marketing plan built around the right pricing strategy. To get your home sold, you need to have a plan for promoting your profile.

How the Wright Brothers Blew It and What It Means for You

The Wright Brothers are often considered a success, and heroes, in our history books. Hardly anybody would ever consider them a failure. In 1903, Orville and Wilbur had built the first powered aircraft that could sustain a controlled flight. These two were innovators for their time and are credited with the invention of the airplane. By many accounts, they were a huge success.

But they're actually failures. They failed. They failed big time. When you dive deeper into their story and their history, you'll see that they blew it. Their life after 1903 can be categorized as a colossal failure. Their name isn't anywhere near the aviation industry.

Compare their company to Ford, which started in 1903, the same year the Wright Brothers experienced flight. In 1913, Henry Ford created the assembly line, making cars affordable to the middle class, and 100+ years later Ford is still around and one of the largest car companies in America and gave birth to Detroit and much of Michigan.

In 1905, the Wright Brothers had a complete monopoly in the aviation industry. They had the world's only working plane, they were the only two pilots who were able to fly it and had a patent that could cover almost any other model plane. They had the tools needed to create and grow a company that was unheard of. Yet, within five years, they were surpassed by competitors at home and abroad.

Their company? Eventually sold and by the time the Golden Age of Aviation came around in the 1920's they were out of business entirely. They could have owned the market and been the leader in aviation but by 1916, the company had been defunct. What happened?

Around 1905, the Wright Brothers were flying in graceful circles over Huffman Prairie, when most planes could barely fly straight and sustain flight. The plane was so far advanced for its time but very few people knew about it. The publicity-shy brothers told nobody about their planes and experiments, so little coverage was made. On top of that, the brothers refused to compete in competitions — which could have established their dominance in the mind of the public — out of fear that their plane's designs would be stolen, even though they had a patent.

When a prospective buyer, mostly the U.S. Department of Defense asked to see the planes fly, they refused to do so without a deposit and instead furnished the names of the limited people who have seen the planes fly. They would then refuse to budge on the price and insist that buyers that the brother's words for it that these planes could fly.

They were afraid of their designs being stolen but at the same time, they didn't worry about the competition. They believed that if they kept their planes a secret, it would take a long time for anybody to design a similar plane.

But keeping the planes a secret didn't help. Eventually the competition did heat up. Specifically, by Glenn Curtiss, who realized that public opinion mattered and would use it against the Wright brothers. He would pilot his inventions in competitions and win awards.

The public came to buy the planes they saw in races, not the Wright brothers' planes, which very few people saw fly. It didn't take long for them to be overtaken. In a fit of irony, by 1929, Curtiss aviation would go on to merge with the last remaining remnants of the Wright brothers' business. But it would come at the cost of having their name second and behind their number one competitor.

There is a lot we can learn from their story. The biggest cause for their failure was their fear and tendency to avoid promoting their planes. Their fear of their ideas being stolen caused them to produce little proof that their planes could fly, so nobody bought them.

Some owners and agents approach home selling like the Wright Brothers. They don't tell anybody about their home. They list it on Zillow and just hope that it will sell. They throw a for sale sign in the yard and expect their home to sell. Secrecy was the biggest downfall of the Wright brothers and it's the biggest cause for many homes not selling.

The outcome of the Wright brothers could have been totally different if they marketed their planes more. If they showed more proof. By the time they did start marketing, it was too late. Competitors had entered the field, and many were tired of the Wright brothers.

You have to promote and market your home from day one. If you wait until you realize that your home isn't selling, it might be too late. Frequency is the key to getting your home sold. It's marketing in every possible channel as often as possible without being annoying. The good part is that you can do it more frequently than a realtor.

For example, if I'm posting a ton of homes for sale on my Facebook page, its kind of gets old after a while. But you could post your home for sale to your friends without it getting old. We're going to explore some of the channels that are available to you and how to get your home sold.

Using Mark Zuckerberg to Sell Your Home: Leveraging the Power of Facebook

Facebook has made it possible for businesses and even homeowners to sell their homes. There are three main ways you can use Facebook to sell your home. First, you can promote your listing on your personal page or a business page, or you can promote your home in various community and garage sale groups in your area, and lastly, you can use Facebook ads to target home buyers and people likely to move.

Have you ever been talking to your friend who you haven't seen in a while, and they suddenly tell you they moved to another part of town? You're probably like, "I had no idea." Maybe you've been on the opposite side, and you're the one who moved without telling your friend. For some reason, when people list their home, they don't tell their friends and family.

Thirty years ago, it was a main way to sell a home. Facebook has given us the ability to tell all of our friends and family, and the people we hardly ever talk to — like the old high-school acquaintance we haven't talked to in 20 years. Traditionally, it would take weeks to tell all of your friends, family, and acquaintance. Now, with just a click of a button, we can share the fact that our home is for sale. And with a click of a button, our friends can tell their friends. This is a powerful way to use Mark Zuckerberg to promote your home. If you post your listing and it gets shared, you will have a significant number of eyeballs on your listing profile.

The second way to use Facebook to promote your home is

through Facebook Groups. I called on a for sale by owner once who managed to sell her home through Facebook groups. Before she even listed her home, she created a series of three posts about her home and said the home was "coming soon." She gained interest in the home and people waited for the posting of the home. When it finally went live, she had an offer in a week and closed a month later.

Facebook groups allow you to target people in the local community and most groups will have thousands of members in them. When using both Facebook groups and your personal page, don't be afraid to post more than once. A small minority of people will see your post. When a group is large, there is a small chance people will see it. So, you can post more frequently. The best part about this is that it's free. The woman who posted her home in the Facebook group paid nothing to have her home marketed and listed. In this case, she saved the full 3% from a seller's commission.

The disadvantage to posting on Facebook is that it can piss people off. Doing one posting isn't likely to make anyone mad but it won't exactly sell your home either. Facebook was invented as a social platform. People don't go on them to buy. They go on to be entertained or connect with people. You have to find a balance between posting your home frequently enough so that you can sell your home and enough so that you don't make people mad.

The other issue with Facebook is that when you do this broad marketing of your home, it's the equivalent to a TV ad. How many times have you watched a commercial that you had zero interest in? Maybe it was a commercial for a catheter when you're only 30. Or it's a commercial for diapers when you don't have kids or they're all adults.

At any given time, only about two percent of people are ready to buy and only ten percent of people are going to move this year. That means for every post you make, it will be irrelevant for 90 percent of people. And only two percent of the people are ready to make a purchase. It's better if you can find a way to target only those 90% of people.

That's what Facebook Ads can be good for. Facebook ads offer the ability to get very specific strangers — allowing you to let people you don't know who are likely to move to learn about your house for sale. For example, you can target people who are looking to downsize and design an ad that is custom built for them and would resonate with them. You could target renters if you want to reach first-time homebuyers. Your options are unlimited.

A local part-time investor I've worked with sells some of his homes through Facebook. When the marketing whizz needed to sell his home, he created an ad that targeted renters within a 20-mile radius of the house. Spending only $5 a day, he had multiple offers within a week and a full price offer that closed on in 30 days.

Using Facebook ads to sell your home is an advanced marketing strategy but I share it with you because if you're serious about getting your home sold without an agent, you will want to try this. First, before you're able to do this, you will need to create a Facebook events page for your home.

Once you do that, you will want to use Facebook's Ad manager to create your ad. There are few terms you need to know before we dive into the exact how to of ads.

- Campaign
- Group
- Ad

A campaign is the highest level of organization. It should hold different target markets. For example, if you plan to market to renters and retired folks, you should create an individual campaign for each. Within each campaign will be your group where you will specify each market. And your ad is where you will hold and create your ads. With the definitions out of the way, let's dive into how to build a powerful Facebook ad that bring buyers. There are 3 components you need to work on:

- Determining your market

- Picking and image
- Writing your copy

First, determine who you want to target. One of my favorite groups is renters. They're often younger and heavily involved on Facebook. I've found great results with them. Next, you want to pick and image. This should be an image of your home. I always like to take the image of a home and overlay it with an element of orange or red so that it contrasts with Facebook. This contrast will make your ad stand out. If you had a blue add, your home would blend in. Lastly, write copy. If you wrote a powerful listing description, you should be able to borrow much of the copy from your listing description.

There is no way I could cover everything you need to know about Facebook ads. Therefore, I recommend looking into Perry Marshall's book on Facebook Ads. It's a great read and has taught me much of what I know about Facebook ads. You can read the book in a weekend and get your ads up and running.

Open Houses: Can They Really Sell Your Home?

There is a lot of debate on whether or not open houses really do anything to sell your home. According to research done by NAR, only 4% of home buyers found and purchased their home from an open house. Among agents, there is a debate if they should even offer them to clients. The return on investment just doesn't seem to be there. Early in career, while I was working as a marketer, I thought open houses were a waste because it couldn't be tied directly to a sale.

An open house might not create a sale directly but will get your home sold. The more experience I got and the more time I dove into open house data, I found something interesting. It turns out that while it doesn't bring in a buyer, often one of the people that came to the open house brought a buyer for us. Done right, an open house can be a great way to tell people about your home, who will go tell their friends or family. The two most common situations came from a neighbor who told their friend or an agent who had another buyer in mind when looking through the house.

The other benefit of an open houses is that you can have a lot of people come through your house without having to schedule any individual tours. It's a great use of your weekend. However, there are things that you do need to look out for. Depending on your house price, you will need to structure your open house differently. The higher priced homes tend to generate super low-quality leads because very people can afford the home and it's a ton of people walking around just wants to see how "the other half" lives.

Open houses, when combined with your other marketing efforts, can be extremely beneficial. It's a great way to get more buyers and exposure to your house. It gives you another thing to advertise. When posting on Facebook we talked about being careful and not wearing down your welcome by being cautious of your posting frequency. If you were posting your home is for sale every time, you would wear out your welcome faster. But when you have an open house, it gives you an excuse to post your home.

To hold an effective open house there are a few rules you should try to follow:

- Hold the open house between 11am and 3pm. These are typically the most popular times.
- Bake some cookies in the oven or pour some vanilla into a bowl and bake it for a few minutes to make the home smell lovely.
- Play some soft music. I'm a fan of J.S. Bach but you can play any classical type song.
- Get rid of any pets if you have them.
- Try to do this in the first week or two — this when ensure the highest traffic amount.

Great. The next issue you have to address is promoting your open house. You can use the ones we already covered like

Facebook to let people know about your open house. You should also be able to update your listing, whether it's listed in the MLS or not, to show that you will be having an open house in the next week.

Just like marketing your home, you will want to market the open house. You want as many people there as possible. It's not enough to just hold the open house and hope that people come. You will need to advertise your home just as much as your actual listing. This is where I really love to use Facebook ads. But another effective strategy is distributing flyers to your neighbors. Take between 50-100 flyers and let your neighbors know that they should come to your open house.

The total cost of an open houses is about $50. On the high end, you could make it about $300 if you wanted to order pizza and food. If you don't want to spend any money or do any marketing for your open house, don't expect to get any results from your efforts.

If you do it right, you should see about 20+ people to come to your open house. For those working in high price points, do a broker only. Either way, a lot of people will be walking through your home so you should have a sign in sheet. This will ensure that people place their information and you can follow them up for feedback on the home, making a reverse offer, and keeping your home safe.

Offline Marketing to Sell Your Home

Offline marketing might be considered old-school, but I find it's one of the best ways to let people know your home is for sale. It's one of the best promotional strategies, in addition to Facebook. For example, one of the classic ways to promote your listing is through postcards. You can deliver "just listed" postcards where you let neighbors know that your home has just been listed.

Now, this may or may not make sense based on the price of your home and how the market is performing. Everyone wants to have a return on investment, so the more expensive your home, the larger the marketing budget. But a lot of the best offline marketing strategies don't really cost any money. Here are two that I recommend the most.

Promote Your Home to Real Estate Agents

The best way to promote your listing, that we found, is to target real estate agents. Specifically, target the top-producing real estate agents. There is an idea, called the 80/20 principle, that states everything is in unequal proportions and distributions.

In real estate, it says that 20 percent of the real estate agents complete 80 percent of the sales. Or, 20 percent of the real estate agents work with 80 percent of the buyers. So, this means that by targeting the 20 percent, we can get in front of 80 percent of the home buyers on the market. In my market, the top 20 percent often consists of around 200 agents, depending on how many real estate agents are in the market at any given time.

There are several ways that we could target real estate agents. My personal favorite our emails and fliers, and then married with Facebook Ads if possible. We love to send email because we can often send two to three emails at zero cost. Then, we will follow it up with a flier because we know that not everybody is going to open and check our email. Lastly, because we have every single real estate agent's email address, we can upload it into Facebook, and they can be targeted with ads. Real estate agents that are working with buyers will know that your home is for sale. This is a great way to get your home sold. While it doesn't get in front of buyers directly, it does help us get it sold. There might be a chance that the real estate agent has a buyer who is a good match for our home.

A second method we use that is separate from our email, flier, and Facebook ads is our Multiple Listing Service. We can set up what's called a reverse prospecting function. This is when we go into our MLS and look for buyers — even if they aren't ours — who may be a good fit for our property.

For example, let's say that we have a three-bedroom home with two-bathrooms for under $150,000. If another agent has a buyer, that they set up a search function that matches this criteria, it will pull the agent's name and send them an email indicating that we have a property their buyer might be interested in. This allows us to market to real estate agents who are most likely to have a buyer that is a good fit for our property that we're trying to sell. As a result, we can increase the probability of finding a home buyer by letting people know or letting real estate agent know that this particular property may fit their buyer's needs.

I find that targeting other real estate agents as one of the best ways that we could promote and distribute with higher success. It tends to be one of our first and primary main focuses, unless of course we have our own internal database that we can access.

Our Own Internal Database

I want to share with you something that is very common in our industry. Many real estate agents will list a home, then start marketing the home to generate potential buyer leads and a home buyer for your home. There are few agents that do marketing to generate home buyers long before they have a home for sale so that when they have a home for sale, they can promote it to the buyer leads they generated over the last few weeks, months, or year.

Every month (at the time of this writing), my company is spending anywhere from $1,000 to $2,000 a month to generate home buyer leads. This way, when we get a listing, we already have a ton of potential and qualified buyers that we can promote a home to. We have home buyers who are looking for a home, we just need a home to sell them.

We keep these leads engaged through sales calls and regularly sending emails to be a resource. Of course, it's not a perfect system and some leads become unengaged over time, but it keeps our database more engaged than it would be otherwise. This allows us to promote our own listings to our own leads and home buyers.

HOW TO SELL ANY HOME... EVEN THE HARD TO SELL HOMES

It's important to understand that not every single real estate agent has or keeps a database of buyer leads that they can promote your home to. When you interview with your real estate agent, this is something that should be addresses in their marketing plan. Does your real estate agent have an active database of buyer leads that they can promote your home to? If not, you lose out on a key channel for getting your listing promoted, and ultimately, sold.

Every Home Requires A Custom Marketing Plan Built Around Standards

"Alex was very easy to work with and very eager to get the job done. Alex took the worry away from selling by being on top of every aspect that came about."

-Clay Hoggard; 2522 Fig Trail

SUCCESS STORY QUICK WINS

About Clay and Katie: Clay accepted a new job with the Battle Creek Police Department and needed to relocate in the next two weeks. Katie and Clay were to be married in

August.

How We Helped Sell Their Home: We took all the steps to create an ideal image of the home. We leveraged professional photos, aerial photos and video to try to get the highest price for the home and sell it in a fast time frame. We also launched a unique and creative marketing campaign targeting other real estate agents in the Jackson area.

Results: In under 30 days we were able to sell the home for $19,000 more than what Clay bought it for less than two years ago.

After accepting a job with the Battle Creek Police Department, Clay needed to quickly sell his house and relocate his family — fiancé and two kids — from Leslie to the Battle Creek area. When Clay reached out to me, he was supposed to start his job in three weeks. This meant he needed his house to sell fast, while still getting top-dollar, or he would be forced to regularly commute from Battle Creek to Leslie every day until his home sold.

But this was the first time Clay and his fiancé, Katie, were selling a house. There were so many uncertainties about the situation. How could they sell their home in Leslie and try to buy a home in Battle Creek at the same time? How long would it take to sell their home? What is the process?

I made sure to simplify the process and explain every step-in detail along the way. I wanted to make sure that they understood everything. "Alex took the worry away from selling by begin on top of every aspect that came about."

Finding and Creating Equity

Clay had previously bought his home in 2016 and that

meant there was minimal equity in the home. There was a small chance that he would have to pay to sell his home rather than getting money back. We knew the challenge we were up against and we wanted to give him the greatest chance of getting some profit from his home, so we created a strong marketing plan. Our goal was to make his home one of the most desirable homes on the market and in the area.

First, we created a strong listing profile — complete with a professional photographer, aerial photos, and a video walk-thru tour. Homes with aerial photos sell 68 percent faster than homes with only traditional photos, according to the MLS. Aerial photography can play a critical role in getting a home sold. It stands out on sites like Zillow, which means your listing will get more views. With a strong listing profile, we knew that we would be able to sell for a higher amount and increase the probability that Clay would have a net profit when he closed. And it paid off.

Selling For $19,000 More Than When He Bought

The listing profile helped a lot. But we also went out of our way to promote Clay's home to every realtor in the area. We decided we would launch a direct-mail campaign targeting real estate agents in Jackson and Lansing. The goal was to promote the home and get some agents to book a showing with their clients, so we sent them a unique letter. One of the pains many real estate agents face in this market is a low-supply of homes so we appealed to this pain with our headline.

Then we sent included a "Fortune Telling Fish" in the envelope that would create a lump in the envelope and create curiosity — improving the odds our letter would get opened. The "Fortune Telling Fish" always told the real estate agent to go tour the property, look it up on the MLS or give me a call. All of our efforts paid off because we were able to sell the home for $19,000 more than he purchased the property just two years ago.

Protecting the Bottom Line

There was a certain net profit I was trying to help Clay get. And I needed to make sure he got that by structuring the offer the right way. The buyer wanted seller's concessions, which is when the seller pays for some of the closing costs. There was a fear that the property wouldn't appraise for the offer price. If it didn't appraise, we would have to try to negotiate again or risk the buyers walking.

In order to protect the net profit, we came up with a provision that would decrease the concessions on a dollar-per-dollar basis of the purchase price. So, if the purchase price had to be reduced by $500 because it didn't appraise, then we would reduce concessions by $500. This protected Clay's bottom line and ensured he would get a profit when he closed on the sale of his home — no matter what the appraisal came in at.

Making Your Promotion Plan

So, what's the best promotional plan to get your home sold? Should you do all of these? Some of these? How much should you spend on each of these? The best promotional plan for you is going to depend on your home.

For example, when we were trying to sell a horse property, we focused more on Facebook ads and less on targeting other real estate agents. That's because few real estate agents have that kind of specialty buyer. Also, we didn't have any buyers we could promote the home to in our database. We've never listed a horse property and we never marketed our business as a horse property expert.

Ultimately, our marketing plan involved using video ads on Facebook, advertising on Google AdWords, and sending marketing material to other horse boarding facilities. This allowed us to get in front of horse owners — the market that was most likely to buy this property.

Making your plan should be done with your real estate agent. They should be able to tell you which marketing channels will be best at getting your home sold. Most of the time, your marketing plan will include all of the methods I laid out in this chapter. The only difference might be how deep you dive on each strategy. For the horse property, we dove deep into Facebook ads. For a property I had listed in Leslie, MI, we dove deep into targeting real estate agents through email and direct-mail.

If your real estate agent doesn't have a marketing plan and you're thinking about relisting with them, you should think again. Without a thoughtful plan for distribution. It's going to be tough to sell your home. This is what we call the list of pray method and it just does not work. At our company, we use a 39-point marketing checklist to make sure we market every single home. We will often customize the plan to suit the home's needs, but our checklist ensures nothing is forgotten.

Now that we looked at the way your listing profile should be built and how to promote, we can shift our focus to hiring a real estate agent. You now have all of the information you need to really judge a real estate agent, rather than relying on how they dress, their smile, or character. While these are important, they don't get a home sold. Let's look at how to hire a real estate agent so you get your home sold this time.

ONE THING

The best way to get your home sold is to target and market to real estate agents that are likely to be working with home buyers.

6 FINDING A REAL ESTATE AGENT

You had your home on the market for some time, and you were disappointed by your real estate agent. Maybe you're thinking and wondering if you should even hire a real estate agent this time around. Maybe you should try to go alone. That's a valid thought, especially if you feel like your real estate agent didn't do anything.

I'm not a big fan of the for-sale-by-owner approach, and that's not just because I'm a real estate agent. It is a viable option for many, but only the few that understand how to market and sell. For example, the person with a background in digital marketing might do pretty well. Also, if you use the TEAM formula, you can get your home sold, too. But there are three main reasons you should think twice about going alone. Here are the benefits of hiring a real estate agent.

AN EASIER PROCESS. There is a big hassle factor when it comes to selling your home. Using a real estate agent is just easier. They can save you hours on the paperwork and legal side of things. From a management perspective, it saves you time that you can devote to doing something else. If you go alone, you need to do all of the paperwork and make sure that you comply with all Federal, State and Local laws. You're on the hook if anything goes wrong.

For example, this means you need to make sure that you have a Seller's Disclosure statement available to buyers at the time of them writing an offer. If not, you could be held legally responsible and a buyer could back out of the agreement. Hiring a real estate agent is just easier. There is also technology a real estate agent has access to which makes the process simple. Instead of having to print, sign and fax paperwork, you can sign all documents with the click of a mouse.

SELL FOR MORE MONEY. This is only a benefit if you hire the right real estate agent. Sure, hiring a mediocre real estate agent might get you the same results as if you went alone. The right real estate agent will get you more money for your home. They will know how to increase the market's perceived value so that you get an offer that is at or above your appraised value. Remember, 20 percent of the real estate agents will do 80 percent of the transactions. The reality is that the right real estate agent has the skill set to sell your home for more money than you could. They are experts in this.

SELL A HOME FASTER. Often, a real estate agent can sell a home faster. A good real estate can build a solid marketing plan built around the right pricing strategy that will get your home sold faster than the other homes on the market. If we can get more people through the door through effective marketing, we can get your home sold faster.

Should I Relist with My Agent?

Loyalty is hard to come by today... There is something to be said about the loyalty some clients have toward their real estate agent. But here's the deal... hiring the same real estate agent without a new plan is a big mistake. I don't care what the reason for hiring the same agent is, it's a mistake if they don't have a new plan. Albert Einstein said, "doing the same thing and expecting a different result is the definition of insanity."

Expecting your real estate agent to sell your home using the same plan — that is if they even have a plan — is insane. It's unrealistic. The solution is quite simple. You either need to fire your real estate agent and look for a new one, or insist that your current real estate agent delivers a formal plan that answers who they will target, how they will market your home for more exposure, their pricing strategy, and how this plan differs from the one they have been operating on since your home was listed with them.

For some, I know firing your real estate agent is a lot easier said than done. There might be a lot of emotions attached to it. Maybe they're family, your friend, or you just feel like you owe them. But if they don't have a new plan, you're going to need to bite the bullet and fire them. The same agent and the same plan is a bad plan for getting your home sold. Luckily, if you didn't resign an agreement with your agent, there isn't much you need to do. You can just let them know you won't be relisting with them. There is no contract you need to try to get out of.

If you plan to hire a new real estate agent, make sure they come to you with a plan. How will they sell your home? What marketing channels will they use to get your home maximum exposure? Who will they target? You will be surprised to learn that there are many real estate agents out there who just kind of wing it. They list the home and hope that it sells. They have no formal plan in place. I typically say real estate agent can be categorized into one of seven levels. A Level 1 real estate agent is someone who lacks a marketing plan, wings it, and lists your home and prays that it sells. They do very little to get your home sold. On the opposite end is a Level 7 real estate agent. They go out with a formal marketing plan and do everything to market your home.

LEVEL 1 AGENT VS. LEVEL 7 AGENT

	Level 1 Agent	Level 7 Agent
Photos	Takes themselves with their cell phone. Quality and dimensions are inconsistent and poor.	Hires a professional and qualified photographer who specializes in real estate photography. Will even get aerial photography when necessary.
Open Houses	Sticks a sign in the yard.	Stick a sign in the yard, sends an email to their database, and invites the neighbors.
Listing Description	Writes basic information about features of the home.	Writes a description that sell the dream of the home. The outcome every home buyer is focused on.
Marketing	Lists it on the MLS.	Puts it on the MLS, optimizes the listing for every website, and looks at other marketing channels like direct-mail and Facebook ads.

So, my question for you is this... what level do you think your real estate agent is? If you plan to relist your home with a new agent, look for an agent who is a Level 7 agent. No marketing plan in place is a sign of a bad agent. Especially if the reason that you're home than themselves marketing based. You don't find yourself in the same position where the issue is marketing and not pricing.

How Do I Find a Real Estate Agent?

If your home didn't sell and you don't plan on hiring the same real estate agent, then there might be a good chance that you need to find a new real estate and don't know where to look. Most people only know one realtor. Once they've used this realtor, they often need to find a real estate agent through other sources. Here are some sources for finding a real estate agent.

Referral Sources Like Friends — Finding an agent through a referral is great. Trust forms the foundation of the relationship you have with your agent. Without it, you will feel like you're being taken advantage of and that your agent doesn't care about you, only the paycheck. About 75 percent of real estate agents get their customers from repeat or referral business, according to the National Association of Realtors.

While finding an agent through referral sources seems like a good idea, it can often backfire. I met a home buyer for coffee who had decided she had enough of her real estate agent and was thinking about hiring me. The real estate agent she was working with was referred to her by someone at work that she deeply trusted. My prospective client had a lot of trust with her agent, but she realized there was a large disconnect. This agent was great, but she was the wrong agent for my prospective client. First, there was the age difference and second, their personalities weren't aligned. This experience is common when it comes to referrals.

That's because what you really want to know is "will MY needs be met by THIS agent?" The traditional referral method doesn't help you answer this question. We're not looking just for the best agent, but the best agent FOR US. And sometimes, that isn't who our friend worked with.

To find the right real estate agent, we have to find an agent that has a solid marketing plan built around the right pricing strategy. The problem is that sellers take the recommendation and just hire the real estate agent. A referral may not be your best option for getting your home sold, but it's a great place to start.

Online Sources — When it comes to finding real estate agents to investigate, that's easy. There are dozens of online tools like Realtor.com, Zillow, Trulia, Coldwell Banker, and many, many more. You can also use Google and type in the "top real estate agent in [your city]". This is great because an agent who can market themselves well online can market your home online. An agent with an online presence will understand how to market their services, and by extension, market your home. There is a good chance that an agent who markets well online will be able to build a solid marketing plan for getting your home sold.

It doesn't matter where you find your real estate agent as long as they have a solid marketing plan built around the right pricing strategy. You could find your agent from a referral, online, or someplace else. It really doesn't matter. Just find someone with a strong marketing plan and the right pricing strategy.

Should I Hire an Agent From A Small Or Big Broker?

I hear this question a lot, should I hire an agent from a small or big broker? There is a belief that an agent from a bigger brokerage will be able to provide you with more resources for getting your home sold. On the other hand, an agent from a small brokerage will be able to devote the time and attention needed to get your home sold.

Here's the deal. I would look less at the broker and more at a real estate agent. The reality is the size of the brokerage will have no bearing on whether your home is sold or not. There are plenty of small brokers that have far better resources to get your home sold than a large broker. And there are many large brokers that can provide the support and attention you need.

It really boils down to the skills and resources that are available to the real estate agent. Not just any resources, but resources that will get your home sold. Often the resources that get a home sold are held by the real estate agent and not the brokerage.

For example, when it comes to promoting a listing, sending an email to a real estate agent's database of buyers is a great way to get a home sold. This database of buyers will always be held by the real estate agent. The real estate agent is responsible for generating their own leads and managing them in database. For that reason, a database of buyer leads is going to be an asset and resource to the real estate agent.

With an agent database of buyers, the broker's resources may be unnecessary and irrelevant. This is why an agent at a small broker may be able to out sell a real estate agent at a big brokerage. Instead of looking at broker size, I recommend looking at the agent's assets and marketing plan described in the last few chapters. I would focus on the resources and assets that the agent has. Many of these will be dependent on the real estate agent and not the broker.

But, Aren't All Real Estate Agents the Same?

It's easy to fall into the thinking that all real estate agents are the same. We all take photos, list the home on the Multiple-Listing Service, and then hope that the home sells. I hope that throughout this book I have revealed there is a difference between real estate agent. It's my hope that while you read this book, you compared all of the strategies we use at the Dolinski Group and the real estate agent you hired to list your home the first time. The reality is that not all agents are the same. They differ in their marketing, philosophy, and their value.

First, agents vary greatly when it comes to their marketing. In an earlier chapter, I revealed the difference between a Level 1 agent and a Level 7 agent. Level 1 agents will typically do the minimum to market a home. On the other hand, a Level 7 agent will go all out on their marketing, and as a result, get a disproportionate amount of results. Some agents will list the home and pray that it sells. Others will promote to their database of buyer leads, send an email to every real estate agent in Lansing, and launch a direct-mail campaign using postcards.

Second, real estate agents differ in their philosophy of selling a home. For example, there are some real estate agents out there that believe it is better to take a listing — even if it's overpriced — than to not take a listing at all. They feel it's better to have your sign in the yard. It's free marketing for them. It's a chance for them to get their name out there. This philosophy shows whether they care or not about getting your home sold.

In our company, we believe listings cost us money and sold homes generate revenue. A sign in your yard is not free marketing. It actually has a very real and high cost for us. We want to get your home sold. If you want to overprice it, we often won't take the listing. We know that from research a solid marketing plan built around the right pricing strategy is what gets a home sold. We care more about getting your home sold and that aligns our objective with a home seller's. They want their home sold and we want their home sold. It's important to understand that every single real estate agent has a different philosophy when it comes to your home. It's important for you to try to reveal that during the interview process.

Third, agent differ in the value they believe they bring. There are many real estate agents out there who will discount their services just to get a listing. I'm a little concerned by that and let me tell you why. A real estate agent who is willing to discount their price is really saying that they don't believe in the value that they have. And that concerns me because isn't your home your most prized possession? Is it one of the most expensive things owned?

I'm not sure that somebody who doesn't believe in the value that they have is somebody who I watch sitting across from the negotiation table. They're timid. This real estate agent has also conveyed that they will do almost anything to get a sale. And when they do almost anything to get a sale, that shows you that they will be willing to negotiate against you and give far more to get this home sold than an agent who believes in their value. You think you're saving money by getting a lower commission, but you're actually losing money because they will sell your home for less. The agent that discounts is more worried about making a quick buck.

Not all real estate agents are the same. They differ in their marketing, their philosophy and their value. You need to try to understand all of these before you hire a real estate agent. Don't make the mistake in assuming that all real estate agents are the same. It certainly appears that way on the outside, but it's far from the truth.

ONE THING

Look for a real estate agent that has a solid marketing plan AND character. Look less at their history and past sales. Past sales do not indicate future success. Look for an agent with a plan for your home.

7 BUILDING YOUR PRICING STRATEGY

Pricing is critically important to getting your home sold, so why wait until the end to talk about it? It's because I didn't want this book to focus on pricing. Often, too many people over emphasize pricing without any real understanding. You see, pricing is in a constant flux. It's not fixed and can move based on the experience you create, your marketing, the real estate agent you hire and the real estate market. There is a big difference between your home's appraised value and your home's market value.

It's our belief that if we take care of marketing and crafting the perfect experience, then pricing a home becomes nearly trivial. We don't have to worry about pricing as much when our marketing and experience are done right and done well. Of course, this doesn't mean we can ignore or neglect pricing, but it becomes an addition to our strategy for getting our home sold rather than our focus. We determine our pricing based on our marketing and experience. Most people will set the price and then determine their marketing and the experience they want to create. Many agents will set a price and then use marketing (or lack thereof) to justify the price. We create our marketing and then use pricing to justify our marketing.

Pricing is important but should never be considered a main focus. Whenever I am listing a home, the last thing we do is talk about pricing. I want to talk about marketing and the experience we can create because all of this will influence our pricing. In this chapter, I want to talk about the dangers of overpricing a home and underpricing a home, and a few pricing strategies based on how the real estate market is doing.

Dangers of Overpricing A Home

The most common danger of overpricing a home is that is doesn't sell, and it sits on the market for a long time. By overpricing a home, you turn away home buyers. I know you may want more for your home and believe that you can always lower the price, but that's just a myth. When you newly list a home, you get an initial wave of interest. There is certain amount the market is willing to pay.

For example, let's say you decide to list your home for $215,000 and all data indicates that the market will only pay $200,000 for your home and its appraised value is at $200,000. In your first 30 days, you will get a wave of interest but no offers.

As your home sits on the market, the amount a buyer is willing to pay creeps down to $197,000. You want to attract more buyers to your home, so you decide to lower the price to $200,000 — the original value the market would have paid. But since your home has been on the market for over 30 days, home buyers wonder what could be wrong with your home. It gets worn by the market and people question why your home hasn't sold.

In order to get your home sold, you will need to drop the price to what the market is willing to pay. This is why some homes don't sell even though keep lowering their price. Their price is still too high compared to what the market is willing to pay. Let's keep looking at the example above. If another 30 days go by and you decide to lower the price to $197,000 but now the market is only willing to pay $195,000, your home still won't sell.

By overpricing your home, you could end up hurting your chance of selling your home or get far less than if you had priced right from the start. When you price too high, you will have to lower the price to what the market is willing to pay. It's a myth that you can always lower the price later and still get a good result. The market and experience tell us otherwise.

In an ideal world, we will set our pricing at the appraised value and then work on using our marketing and experience to make sure we can get that price. This ensures you get the most amount of money for your home without risking a deal falling apart. So, we need to watch out for overpricing our home.

Dangers of Underpricing A Home

Just as it's dangerous to overprice a home, it's dangerous to underprice a home. Underpricing a home can cause two issues. First, by underpricing, you're leaving money on the table. You're not getting as much for your home as you could have. Second, underpricing your home too far may actually hurt your chances at getting your home sold.

If you underprice your home too far, home buyers will think there is something seriously wrong with your home. If your home is worth $250,000 and you're selling it for $230,000, home buyers are going to question your motivation. While you might be doing it to get rid of it fast, a home buyer might think there is something wrong with the home. As a result, they may stay away from it.

So even though you underpriced your home, by doing so, you pushed the market perception of the home lower. For example, by pricing your home at $230,000 a buyer might only pay $220,000 for your home because they believe there is a risk. The extra $10,000 will cover the difference in case they find something wrong with your home.

We want to make sure that we are setting our pricing right. We can underprice it to get it sold faster, but if we go too low, we risk not selling the home at all. That's not a position you want to be in. If you later try to raise the price, you will have to justify the price increase.

How To Determine A Home's Exact Value

A home's value is determined by two economic principles: a determination of value — typically referred to as a comparative market analysis or home value analysis — and market dynamics. These two principles provide the foundation we need to understand the value of a home. We're going to dive deep into how to perform a home value analysis (HVA) to determine the value of a home and then look at some of the market dynamics and forces that will help us shape our price.

When a real estate transaction takes place, two things are revealed: what a buyer is willing to pay for a specific home and what a seller is willing to sell it for. If we take a high number of completed transactions in a short period of time, then we can determine with a high level of accuracy what a buyer is willing to pay for a specific home and the amount for which a seller is willing to sell any home by comparing it to the past sales.

Said another way, the price of a home can determined by comparing similar homes — location, style, size, etc. — that sold in the last three to six months to the home that you want to buy. In a homogeneous neighborhood with a high density of homes selling in a short period of time, determining the home's value is relatively easy.

For example, if there is a 150-condo complex where four similar units — same bedrooms, baths, and square footage — sold in the last six months, we can determine the value of any other condo unit in the complex by averaging the sale price of three or more of the condo units. Let's say you want to sell Condo A and you're wondering what to price it at. Condo B, C, and D sold for $200,000, $205,000, and $204,000, respectively. We can get the average by taking the sum and dividing it by the number of units. In our case, the total is $609,000. When divided by the number of units, three, we get an average price of

$203,000. So, when determining our price, we should start around $203,000.

The key to determining a price through a home value analysis is finding comparable homes. As long as we're in areas that are densely populated and homogenous, we can price with confidence. The type of areas that tend to fit this description are condos and larger subdivisions, like Mayberry communities.

Picking Your Comparables. In our condo example, finding the comparable homes was easy. We simply picked other units in the condo complex. No matter the home you want to buy, the principle is the same, start by finding very similar homes to yours that sold in the last three to six months. We will refer to these very similar homes as comparables moving forward. These are the three rules to we use to find good comparables.

Rule #1: Pick the same style. For example, if you're looking to sell a condo, you should compare your home to other condos. If you're looking to sell a cape-cod in downtown Lansing, you should find other cape-cods.

Rule #2: Location, location, location. Select homes that are as close to the address of the home you're selling. Try to use homes that are within a quarter- to a half-mile. In rural areas, you may have to expand this to a mile or two. For example, if you're thinking about buying a home in Allison Oaks in Lansing, then you should use homes in Allison Oaks. You shouldn't be looking at homes in Okemos. However, there are exceptions to the rule. For example, a home might be around the block, but be in a different school district.

Rule #3: Within 10 percent of square footage. For example, if you're thinking about selling a home that is 2,000 square feet, all of the homes that you pick should be within 1,800 and 2,200 square feet (2,000 − [2,000 *10%]) or (2,000 + [2,000 *10%]). If you follow this process, you will have a small number of homes to use as comparables. There is a high chance that you have more than three, so you will need to look through the homes to find the best three.

This is a subjective decision, but they should be as close to the home you're selling. Good ways to filter further are through bedroom count (make them the same), condition of the interior, and the number of bathrooms. But what if you can't find three exactly similar properties? Maybe it's in a different school district, the square footage is off, it doesn't have a garage, the basement is finished, or any number of things.

It's rarely the case that we find homes that are exactly similar. Often homes have an extra bathroom, more or less square footage, finished basements or not, and other amenities, like a deck. What do we do then? We still select these homes, but if we took the average there is likely to be a higher margin of error. Meaning, we won't be able to rely on the value we determine. It's no better than just picking a fixed percentage below asking. To account for these differences, we make what we call "adjustments."

Making Adjustments to a Home. Adjustments are made to properties to correct for minor differences in comparable homes. Most adjustments are considered "opinion." This is the art part of finding how much a home is worth. It's this subjective opinion that causes appraisers to come up with different values for your home. For example, if the home you want to sell has 2,000 square feet and a comparable home has 2,100 square feet, we should consider making an adjustment to the comparable property. As a rule of thumb, adjustments should ONLY apply to our comparable properties NOT the home we're considering buying.

Depending on the features — positive or negative — we may make a positive or negative adjustment. If a comparable lacks something that the home we are selling, then we will make a positive adjustment. The opposite is true for features our comparables have. For example, if a $200,000 comparable lacks a deck but the home we are selling has one, we would add $5,000 (chosen adjusted value for deck) to the comparable sale price. Giving us a new sale price of $205,000.

The more adjustments that are needed for our comparables, the less confident we can be in our pricing and the larger the variation. Meaning, if you hired 3 different appraisers and many adjustments are needed, you're likely to see three very different results.

The Effect of Market Dynamics. Once we've picked our comparables and made adjustments, we need to understand where the market is and where it's heading. Let's explore this topic further and talk about some of the pricing strategies based on our market.

Pricing Strategies for Different Markets

We've looked at how our TEAM formula can influence the price our home sells at, and we even talked about how to find your home's appraised value. What we haven't looked at is how to set your pricing strategy based on the current market conditions, specifically how should we price in a seller's market and a buyer's market? From research and experience, we should have very different pricing strategies for these markets.

In a seller's market, your pricing strategy should be less on the market comparables and more on the future value. When house prices are on the rise fast, going back and looking at comparables can be less accurate. You will want to try to look at current homes on the market. For example, what are the current asking price for homes on the market that are similar to yours. We can often price above our appraised value because by the time it sells, the market value is going to be higher.

Even if we make a small mistake, the market will often correct us. For example, assume your home is worth $210,000 when it is listed, and we list it at $220,000. Two months go by and it hasn't sold. With house prices rising, we keep the price where it is. In another month it sells for $220,000. In a seller's market, we can get away with pricing high because the market will eventually reach that price — within reason of course.

In a buyer's market, we need to price ahead of the market, or we risk running into issues. It's a buyer's market where overpricing your home can cost you dearly. To price your home, you will look at comparables, then set your price lower than those comparables so that you price ahead of the market.

Let me explain why it's important to price ahead of the market. Say you list your home on the market for $200,000. It's worth about $195,000 at the time of listing your home. Home values are dropping by about one percent every single month. It's taking six months for a home to sell, on average. Four months go by and your home's value is now $187,316 — roughly.

You realize you need to drop your home's price, but you only drop it to $190,000. You're still below what the market will pay and you're still behind the market. If you let another three months go by, your home's value drops to $181,752. The only way to prevent this is by getting ahead of the market. If you originally had listed your home near $190,000, you would have sold it in four to five months and maximized your earnings.

To get your home sold in a buyer's market, you need to price ahead of the market, and that often means pricing below market comparables. In a seller's market, you can often price above the comparables. The market will often catch up and fix any pricing mistakes made — within reason.

ONE THING

Price your home based on your marketing, the experience you create, and the market dynamics. Don't neglect or argue with the market if you want your home sold.

8 A SPECIAL INVITATION

Discover How Homeowners in Your Neighborhood Are Moving to the Home of Their Dreams By Turning Their "Expired Listing" into "Just Solds" and How YOU Can Join Them Too.

To sell your home, you need one thing to be present. Without it, you might as well take down the for-sale sign and take your listing off Zillow because it will be difficult to get your home sold. What's the one thing you need to be present...?

... A motivated buyer.

That's it. Without a motivated buyer, it's a monumental task to sell your home for top dollar and in days or weeks. A motivated buyer buys. It's that simple. Motivated buyers have a strong desire or need to buy — often because of divorce, retirement, relocation, or something else.

Your goal — or your real estate agent's goal — should be to get TONS of qualified and motivated home buyers through your front door to tour your home. If you can get motivated buyers to look at your home, then you can:

- Sell your home faster and for more than all of the other homes on the market, even if your home isn't in the "most desirable" neighborhood or doesn't have the

"most desirable" layout.
- Have multiple offers on the negotiation table and pick ONLY the best one that gets you the exact terms you want for selling your home.
- Stop wasting time with tire kickers and show your home to qualified and motivated home buyers.

Motivated buyers change the game of selling. If you can generate enough motivated buyers, you don't have to wonder why your home has had few showings. No more leaving your home at 6:30pm to let home buyers, who will never buy because they haven't talked to a lender, tour your home.

It's possible to find enough motivated buyers in any market to sell your home for more and faster than the competition… even in the worst markets, like those of 2008 through 2012. I know this to be true because homes, that weren't foreclosures or short sales, still sold.

The homes that sold all had one thing in common. This is the secret that few homeowners and realtors ever realize. They all had a solid marketing plan built around the right pricing strategy that brought in TONS of motivated buyers.

WHY SHOULD YOU LISTEN TO WHAT I HAVE TO SAY ABOUT SELLING YOUR HOME?

Hi, I'm Alex Craig, the founder of the Dolinski Group and a local Lansing real estate agent with Coldwell Banker Hubbell-BriarWood. Over the last decade, I became a highly-paid independent marketing consultant for companies in the Telematics industry that sold to Fortune-500's.

In 2016, I decided to close down my business and transition into real estate. I wanted to use my marketing skills and knowledge to help homeowners, like yourself, get more exposure for their home, more showings, more offers, and ultimately, get their home sold for more and faster. When I looked into the real estate industry, I noticed it was filled with a lot of "list and pray" agents. They stick a sign in your yard, list it on the multiple-listing service, and then pray that another agent brings a qualified home buyer.

It seemed to me that few real estate agents knew how to market a home for sale and generate qualified and motivated buyers. Instead, it looked like many real estate agents knew how to get a home listed but had limited skills in getting a home sold. And I got tired of this, so I jumped into the industry. I wanted to bring a new standard when it came to the marketing done for a client's home. I have used my skills to market a client's home in every available marketing channel possible — from direct-mail postcards and letters, to Facebook Ads, to Google Search Engine Ads.

I have been able to help homeowners get their home sold, where other agents have failed. For example, in the Summer of 2018, I was able to sell a horse farm property in 3+ months and had over 18 showings. Previously, the home sat on the market with a "list and pray" agent for 5 months and had only 3 showings.

I have helped many homeowners in these similar situations. If you find yourself in this kind of situation — long time on the market, few showings, and an unsold home, then you will benefit from using the Dolinski Group to sell your home.

"I PLAN TO HIRE MY AGENT AGAIN"

I can honestly say that I appreciate that kind of loyalty. There is something to be said about loyalty in today's society. From talking with homeowners, they often tell me they feel like they owe their real estate agent to relist because their agent just spent money and time trying to get the home sold. Or they made a promise to their real estate agent and feel like they can't go back on their word. Let me ask you something though...

... if your agent hasn't been able to sell your home while

they've had it listed, do you think they will be able to sell it in the next six months?

Albert Einstein said, "doing the same thing and expecting different results is the definition of insanity." I appreciate the loyalty and your concern for the well-being of your agent, but what about yours? What about getting your home sold?

If your goal is to sell your home, you owe it to yourself to look at all of your options. I know my client, Becky Turner, who sold her home after firing her previous agent and hiring us, was glad she looked at all of her options. It's easy to fall into the trap believing that all real estate agents are the same and the only difference is whether we know them or not. We all market and sell homes, but the effort we make is where we all differ.

Real estate agents can usually be categorized into one of seven levels. A Level 1 real estate agent is a "list and pray" agent. They do as little as possible to get a home sold. A Level 7 real estate agent goes all out and markets the home on every available channel.

So, my question for you is this... what level do you think your real estate agent is? If your agent is a 7th level agent, then by all means, hire them again. Throw this letter in the trash and ignore what I'm saying. Otherwise, I recommend that you keep reading to learn how you can hire a 7th level real estate agent to get your home sold.

SELL YOUR HOME THIS TIME WITH EXPERT MARKETING BUILT AROUND A SOLID PRICING STRATEGY, THE PERFECT FORMULA FOR SELLING YOUR HOME

I have spent the last decade and nearly $500,000 in marketing budget to help my clients sell and market their services. I'm taking those same skills I built and applying them to the real estate industry.

The Dolinski Group spends over $1,000/month marketing to generate home buyers and get our clients' homes sold. Some agents take a listing and then work to find a buyer. We actively market for buyers every single month. So, when we get a listing, we can instantly promote our listing to all of the buyer leads we have generated over the last year. We are constantly looking to drive leads to our websites through Facebook, direct-mail, and more.

We've also developed our Ultimate 37-Point Marketing Checklist, which includes the basics, like getting photos taken by a professional real estate photographer and listing your home in the multiple-listing service, and more advanced tasks, like evaluating the need for aerial photography, create a video tour with photos to be hosted on YouTube, and emailing top agents in Lansing — ones that are actually working with home buyers.

Our experienced marketing results in more showings, more offers, and more qualified buyers than the average home on the market. Ultimately, you're able to beat the competition and get your home sold faster and for more.

Stop fighting the same challenges. You can get your home sold with a strong marketing plan built around a solid pricing strategy. You can finally sell your home and move to your dream home. You can get down to Florida for your retirement. You can move into the bigger home, so your family isn't on top of each other and running out of space. You can finally stop paying two mortgages.

THE DOLINSKI GROUP'S SERVICES ARE UNIQUE IN A FEW WAYS:

- At our disposal, we have the ability to market better than most real estate agents. We know how to use marketing channels like direct-mail, social media, and video to get your home sold.
- We care more about getting your home sold than getting it listed. Our goal is the same as yours: get your home sold. We believe that listings cost us money and sold homes are better as they generate revenue for our business.
- We have the backing of one of THE largest real estate brokers in Lansing and Michigan. Coldwell Banker Hubbell-BriarWood is one of the nation's top Coldwell Banker Franchises. You get access to these resources, too.

INTRODUCING THE DOLINSKI GROUP REAL ESTATE SERVICES FOR HOME SELLERS WHO COULDN'T SELL THEIR HOME BUT WANT TO

The Dolinski Group real estate services is a full-service agency to help home sellers sell their homes when other agents have failed. We take care of everything from listing to closing, but we have focused our efforts on creating some of the best and world-class marketing. It includes access to the right pricing strategy and our Ultimate 37-Point Marketing Checklist to help get your home sold. Here is the aim of our pricing and marketing plan:

- Get TONS of qualified and ready-to-go home buyers with pre-approval letters practically begging their agent to tour your home.

- Circumvent the competition so you don't drown in the sea of thousands of other homes for sale on the market. Hint: it involves using Facebook Ads and marketing where nobody else is.
- Increase the perceived value of your home so the amount the market is willing to pay is as high as it can be. This way, you can net the most amount of money in your pocket. It starts with the right positioning and creating the right experience.
- Use new marketing like social media to go where home buyers are... online. 90% of home buyers start their search online, yet most marketing is focused offline.
- A systematic marketing plan that ensure we don't forget anything, you get maximum exposure for your home, and ultimately, get the highest price.

One of the things that we've learned from testing and experience is that if we can optimize our pricing and marketing, then everything else will pretty much take care of itself. For example, negotiating becomes virtually unnecessary because you have other interested and qualified home buyers who want to write offers on your home or tour it.

Here's what you get with our services:

HOME VALUE ANALYSIS REPORT

Pricing right from the start matters. If you want to sell your home for the highest price possible, we need to price it right. It's counterintuitive, I know. Without services, I or my team will do a home value analysis to determine the best pricing for getting your home sold. First, we do exactly the work of an appraiser to find your home's potential value. The difference is that an appraiser will sometimes charge $400 or more for this service.

Once we have an idea of the potential value, we look at factors that could influence the price you will be able to sell at. For example, what direction is the real estate market headed? What are the current conditions? How long has your home been on the market before? This ensures that we price right from the start and your home doesn't sit on the market. It also ensures that we don't run into appraisal and financing issues with the home buyer.

37-POINT MARKETING BUILT TO DRIVE HOME BUYERS

In addition to our company's regular marketing to drive home buyer leads, we will put into place our Ultimate 37-Point Marketing Checklist to drive the most amount of home buyers leads to your home as possible.

We take our Ultimate Marketing Checklist and customize to your home as needed. For example, if you have a special property, we will explore other marketing plans to get your home sold. Each marketing channel we use has been tested with other homeowners and we've used them in the past to get homes sold. On our staff are some of the best marketers in the country — from myself to other independent contractors I commission to help create ads and other marketing material.

Our marketing checklist focuses on optimizing everything digitally. That's because most home buyers are online searching for homes. We want to be where all of the home buyers are.

FORGET THE REST SYSTEM

We work really hard to make selling your home easy for you. That means once we have an offer, we do our best to coordinate all of the logistics on your behalf until the time of closing. This means handling everything with the title company and appraiser so that you can forget about it until the time of closing. Sound fair? Good.

"We're Going to Wait Until…"

... Next season. Next Winter. Next year. It seems logical to wait. You had your home listed for the last six months or more, and you're tired. You're tired of showings and having the for-sale sign in your yard. It makes sense to try to give your home some time to cool off and reintroduce it into the market later so you can get more interest. That said, if I presented you an offer tomorrow at full asking price... would you still wait to sell your home?

Here's my solution. Take advantage of our 60-Day Easy Exit Listing Addendum. Let us get your home listed and see what we can do in the next 60 days. If you're not happy with the results, then we can take your home off the market and wait until you're ready. It's only 60 days. What if you could get your home sold in those 60 days? Our Ultimate Marketing Checklist is designed to generate new interest in your home no matter how long it has been listed on the market.

"I Want to Finish Some Projects First"

Makes perfect sense. Totally understandable. We want your house looking the best it can. Here is a question for you... how do you know which projects are important and what will get the home sold?

You might be surprised to learn how little some things matter to home buyers. Something you think they care about isn't something they care about at all. But we never know until we market test the home.

Here's what I recommend... Let's get your home back on the market and get people seeing it. We can get real estate agents and brokers to provide feedback on the home. After every home tour, we send a survey asking for feedback. Our questions are designed to get responses about what people like about your home and hate about it.

When we do this, we get feedback on what projects are needed, what ones we can skip, and how to position your home. When we find what people love about your home, we can emphasize that and overcome objections home buyers have for your home.

"We're Not Putting It Back on The Market"

I appreciate the fact that you might have decided to not put your home back on the market. Let me ask you a quick question. If there was a buyer for your home, the perfect, non-contingent, pre-approved, great buyers, and this buyer would pay you asking price and close in 60 days or less, you would at least consider selling your home to this buyer, wouldn't you?

I would hope so. Again, give us 60 days to list your home and see what we can do. See what our marketing can do to get your home sold. It's only 60 days and no risk for you.

If you're unhappy with our marketing, then you can cancel our agreement. At least you can rest without worry knowing that you did everything you could.

"We're Going to List with The Same Agent"

Okay, I totally understand that. And I can really appreciate that loyalty. Can I ask you a tough question? Why do you think you'll get a different result doing the same thing? What is your agent planning on doing differently this time?

I get it. I know a lot of people who relist with their agent do it because they feel like they owe them. They spent money and time getting their home sold.

But here's an idea… if you have 15 minutes, let me give you a second opinion on selling your home for more money and fewer headaches.

"Will You Cut Your Commission? Other Agents Will."

There are a lot of agents out there who are willing to cut their commission to less than 6% and I'm a little concerned by that. Let me tell you why...

Do you feel like you own anything more valuable than your home? Could you say that your home is one of your most valuable possessions?

If an agent is desperate that they are willing to broadcast the fact that they don't think they have value as a Realtor, then I'm confused and concerned for you.

Is that the type of person you want sitting across from the negotiating table trying to negotiate you a better price? We are talking about a person who has already admitted that he or she doesn't even see value in himself or herself.

They also have communicated that they are desperate to make the "sale". Do you think they are going to be more worried about closing the deal or getting you the best outcome for your home? Is that the type of person you want to represent you in the most valuable transaction of your life?

If that's what you're looking for, then we're probably not a good fit. Considering we spend thousands of dollars a month on marketing generating buyer leads, and I have spent the last decade as a highly-paid marketer, which will help get your home sold, that's very valuable. This an opportunity for you to finally get your home sold though.

WHAT OUR CLIENTS ARE SAYING ABOUT US...

"Alex Craig is a pleasure to work with! He is organized, conscientious, and we feel like we made a friend after working with him. Such a hard worker! He was willing to go to great lengths to help us sell our house. We can't say enough good things about him! The next time we need the services of a real estate agent, Alex will be the only one we'll call. We will be sure to recommend him to family and friends!"

-Sue Goodenow

"Alex was very easy to work with and very eager to get the job done. Alex took the worry away from selling by being on top of every aspect that came about."

-Clay Hoggard

"To find a realtor who does not pressure their clients into a sale to make a quick dollar is hard to come by. You will not be pressured by Alex. He will assist you with the decision making, but ultimately leaves the decisions to you. I highly recommend Alex, not just for his trustworthiness as a professional, but to also have a good friendly relationship with his clients. He is prompt with following back with his clients as well. He listened to our needs and was able to show us homes within our budget. Our overall experience with Alex has been fantastic, and I feel comfortable giving him 5 stars knowing he will be able to assist you as well."

-Holly F.

"We chose Alex to be our real estate agent to buy and sell based on his website profile. He's a great fun guy that is very passionate about his job. His communication is on point, he is always quick to respond to a call or text and we always felt we knew where exactly we were in the buying process. Before our closing he double checked all our documentation and found an error on part of our bank. In the end we received money back due to this error that Alex found. We would highly recommend him to anyone looking to buy/sell!"

-Kari Larson

"Alex is bright and personable. He has had tons of ideas to help us get our home sold. Very approachable and replies to questions quickly. We are very happy with Alex and will recommend him to everyone we know!"

-Becky T.

"I feel so very fortunate to have worked with Alex. As a first-time homebuyer who had never worked with a realtor, I trusted the reviews I read online and I am glad I did! I had a unique situation- I had to find and close on a home within ~2.5 months. He recognized the urgency of my situation and was willing to help. Alex is an excellent communicator and is readily accessible. I appreciate that he communicates via text message because that is easier for me with work. He always answered questions in a way that was easy to understand. Alex was ready to show me any home I wanted to look at and pointed out things about them I would not have thought about. Once I found "the one", he worked really hard to make sure I did not overpay and gave me great tips to make the process as smooth as possible. He has a very easygoing personality and you can tell he cares about his clients and has a passion for his work! I never felt pressured or rushed into anything. If I ever need to move/buy/sell in the future, I will not hesitate to contact him! I would recommend him to all of my friends and family. Thanks for the awesome experience Alex!"

-Amanda Petrovsky

"I am a person who does not write a lot of reviews but please see below because Alex has done everything to earn this stellar review. Alex is a rare find and we were lucky enough to have him as our realtor. Work Ethic, Integrity, Trustworthy, Capable and Resilient are some words that come to mind. He is eclectic in his approach and somehow made this process calm and very easy especially in the highly competitive Okemos housing market. You could read 100 reviews and they will all tell you the same thing about Alex, he knows what he is doing and is a great person. What we want to make clear is that Alex will stick it out with you even when the going gets tough. He helped us find a house in a very competitive market. Alex navigated us for s through the craziness of constant contract changes, inspections, figuring out potential renovation costs, and continuous doubt about whether we would actually ever close. Throughout the process he kept us informed and led us as a team. He was truly amazing. We feel like we could happily go on and on about Alex. But to cut straight to it, we want to say that Alex will always be a special person to our family. When we so often over the years didn't think it would be possible, he helped us secure a permanent home in Okemos. Thank you!"

-Brad, Lisa, and Etta Bean

WHAT TO DO NOW?

If you're ready to get your home sold, here's what you can expect next. When you get in touch with us, we will schedule a time with you to come over to have a look at your home so we can do a home value analysis and have a 15-minute conversation about what we will do to market and sell your home, and go over why you think your home didn't sell yet.

This is purely for exploratory purposes to make sure that we are a good fit together and there is no commitment at this point. You won't be asked to sign anything. If you're ready of course, we can take care of it at that time.

We aren't going to "pitch" you on our services. We want to answer only the questions, "What are we going to do to sell your home?" It's about the specific actions we will take and what you can expect once we sign an agreement together. Not about how good I am or how many homes I have sold.

You can get in touch with us in a few ways to set up our 15-minute appointment.

- Send a personal email to me Alex Craig at alexc@cb-hb.com. Use the title "Expired Listing" and I will be in touch with you to schedule an appointment to get together
- You can also call me or text me at my personal cell phone at 734-752-2496.

To Selling Your Home,

Alex Craig

ONE LAST THING

You have the opportunity to get your home sold by using a strong marketing and pricing plan that generates motivated buyers. You can decide to list your home and hope that you can time the market. Hope that the spring or a few months from now will have more buyers. You can list with the same real estate agent and hope that they sell your home this time around.

Or you can work with a real estate agent that has an Ultimate Marketing Checklist and will build a strong pricing strategy so you can generate motivated buyers and ultimately get your home sold in weeks. Not months.

So, what's it going to be? The choice is yours.

ABOUT THE AUTHOR

I'm Alex Craig, the founder of the Dolinski Group, a real estate agency team part of Coldwell Banker Hubbell-BriarWood in Lansing, Michigan (at the time of this writing). I have been using my marketing skills and knowledge to help homeowners, like yourself, get more exposure for their home, showings, more offers, and ultimately, get their home sold for more and faster than other real estate agents. I have used my skills to market clients' homes in every available marketing channel possible — from direct-mail, to Facebook Ads, to Google AdWords. All of this has allowed me to sell homes where other real estate agents have failed.

FOR SELLING YOUR HOME, CONTACT THE DOLINSKI GROUP AT: 734-752-2496 or EMAIL ALEXC@CB-HB.COM

www.ingramcontent.com/pod-product-compliance
Lightning Source LLC
Chambersburg PA
CBHW020431220526
45464CB00002B/663